KEY TEXTS

THOEMMES

Printed in England by Antony Rowe Ltd.

KEY TEXTS
Classic Studies in the History of Ideas

CHURCHES IN THE
MODERN STATE

John Neville Figgis

THOEMMES
PRESS

This edition published by Thoemmes Press, 1997

Thoemmes Press
11 Great George Street
Bristol BS1 5RR, England

US office: Distribution and Marketing
22883 Quicksilver Drive
Dulles, Virginia 20166, USA

ISBN 1 85506 543 6

This is a reprint of the 1914 edition

Publisher's Note

CHURCHES IN THE MODERN STATE

BY

JOHN NEVILLE FIGGIS
LITT. D., HON. D.D. (GLASGOW)
OF THE COMMUNITY OF THE RESURRECTION
HONORARY FELLOW OF ST. CATHARINE'S COLLEGE, CAMBRIDGE

SECOND EDITION

LONGMANS, GREEN AND CO.
39 PATERNOSTER ROW, LONDON
NEW YORK, BOMBAY, AND CALCUTTA
1914

THOMAE · ALEXANDRO · LACEY
MAGISTRO · DISCIPULUS
SCRIPTOR · INDIGNUS

J. N. F.

HUNC · LIBRUM
PIGNUS · AMORIS
DEDICAT

PREFACE

THE four lectures which make the main matter of this volume were delivered to the clergy in Gloucester in June 1911 at the request of the Bishop of the Diocese. Since then I have re-written them, still, however, retaining the lecture form. Pressure of other work is responsible for so long a delay in publication. The first Appendix contains a paper read to the Royal Historical Society, and printed in the Society's *Transactions*. This develops in greater detail the historical thesis which is the basis of the lecture on "The Great Leviathan." The other Appendix consists of three articles on Creighton, Maitland, and Acton, which were contributed by the author to the *Guardian* in the year 1907. Since they deal to some extent with the main topic of these lectures, I have ventured to in-

clude them, with the kind permission of
the Editor.

One or two further words may elucidate
the meaning of the volume. The word
" Churches " in the title-page is used
without any theological prejudices to denote religious bodies of any kind. In
regard to the latter part of the lecture
on " The Civic Standpoint," should any
reader be disposed to charge the writer with
inculcating a cowardly attitude in the face
of industrial oppression, I would ask him
to read alongside of it the two sermons for
Ash Wednesday and the Friday succeeding,
printed in *Antichrist*.[1] In regard to the
first Appendix, I would wish here to accept
the correction suggested by Mr. C. N.
Sidney - Woolf in his valuable work on
Bartolus. I have no doubt at all that
he is right in the importance which he
attaches in the development of ideas to the
enthusiasm of the twelfth-century lawyers.

[1] *Antichrist and Other Sermons.* London : Longmans,
Green & Co.

In the chapter on " Ultramontanism," I trust that nothing has been said which can wound the religious sense of other Christians. It is of the political meaning of an ecclesiastical autocracy that I am speaking. Further, in claiming inherent life for the different parts of the Catholic Church, the writer is not to be understood as meaning by that an absolutely independent entity possessed by the Church of England.

The main purpose of the lectures, slight though they be, will have been accomplished if I can have persuaded the reader to see that the problem is one which is concerned not with ecclesiastical pretensions so much as with the nature of human life in society. Special conditions are bringing this matter to the fore from directions far different. No ideal of " the great State " will ultimately succeed in doing the good anticipated if its founders ignore the fundamental facts of the reality of small societies. The author has been led to his present views not by the desire to defend Church rights, but by long brooding over the Austinian doctrine and the perception forced on him at last through Maitland and Gierke, that it is either fallacious or so profoundly inadequate as to have no more than a verbal justification. One begins by thinking Austin self-evident, one learns that many qualifications have to be made, and finally one ends by treating his whole method as abstract and theoretic.

So far as this side of the question goes, the writer can claim that what is here set down embodies the main results of more than twenty years' study. For ever since I began, in 1891, to study the divine right of kings, I have devoted such time as could be spared from other and more immediate claims to the study of those writers in many ages who were concerned with the problems of political philosophy, and more especially with that class of problems discussed in this volume. I know how incomplete and sketchy what is here written down must appear. But I would beg the reader to bear in mind that if its expression is hasty, this is not the result either of indolent levity or of a desire to promote a clericalist cause. I have come to different notions about the juristic nature of the State, the Church, and the individual from those which seemed at one time so clear. If once people understand that we are concerned with the profoundest of all the problems of men's life together, they will be less ready to condemn or to support opinions on any narrow ground.

I have to thank Messrs. Macniven and Wallace, Edinburgh, for their kind permission to make citations from *The Free Church of Scotland Appeals*, 1903, edited by Mr. R. L. Orr.

I have further to thank the Rev. A. Wicksteed for much advice in correcting the proof-sheets, and the Rev. Lionel Thornton for compiling the Index.

J. NEVILLE FIGGIS.

CONTENTS

LECTURE I

CHURCHES IN THE MODERN STATE

CHURCHES IN THE MODERN STATE

LECTURE I

A FREE CHURCH IN A FREE STATE

Libera Chiesa in Libero Stato.   Such is the
aphorism in which the maker of Italian unity
summed up the ideal of statesmanship for
the solution of the perennial problem of the
two powers.   Whether or no this ideal can
be attained is doubtful; that it never has
been attained is certain.   But approximations
may be made.   Mr. Gladstone used to say
that political ideals were never realised.
That may be true, but it does not follow
that they are never effective.   Christian
holiness is not only never achieved in
perfection, but it is far less nearly and
less frequently achieved than the ethical
ideals of Pagans or Mohammedans.   Yet
for all that it leads to a life higher, not
merely in degree but in kind, than that of

all other moral or religious systems. And so I think that we may spend some time, not unprofitably, in discussing what we mean by claiming freedom for the Church; whether, politically speaking, there is such an entity as a Church; and what, if so, is the least that it can claim without committing corporate suicide.

It is "the least that it can claim" of which we are to speak. Some, perhaps, will doubtless criticise what is here said, especially in the third lecture, and will complain that it is unduly conciliatory to the State. I cannot help that. That the Church might under certain conditions claim a great deal more may be true. But with so much frank denial of her right to claim anything at all, it seems to me at this juncture far more profitable to discuss what she must claim so long as she is a Church, than what she might claim if her right to an inherent life were once universally admitted by statesmen and lawyers.

First of all, then, it seems needful to make clear that the very notion of the Church as an independent entity is denied explicitly or implicitly in much of the current controversial writing, and is surrendered too often even by her own representatives. I do not say that we are as yet face to face with any such denial, official and public. But we are face to face with it as a current presupposition and as a definite theory. For instance, in one of the hearings of the case of Canon Thompson, Mr. Justice Darling delivered himself to the effect that a Law of God had been altered by an Act of Parliament.[1] This, it is true, was only an *obiter dictum*: all he was actually adjudicating upon was the question, whether in view of certain words in the Deceased Wife's Sister's Act a writ of prohibition might lie against the Dean of Arches. No one disputes his competence to interpret the Act of Parliament, or need complain

---

[1] " For my part, I am of opinion that this marriage, which before was contrary to the Law of God merely because the statute condemned it as such, is so no longer, and that by virtue of the statute which legalises it. For otherwise, we should have here a declaration that statutes recognise a certain contract as continuing contrary to the Law of God, and do yet enact that it shall be good by the Law of England." Why should they not?—*Law Reports, Probate Division,* 1910, p. 81.

of the House of Lords for upholding his interpretation. Nobody disputes that if the highest judicial authority declared that Parliament meant white when it said black, that dictum would be law unless repealed. But the fact remains that Mr. Justice Darling used those words, and that they express in a piquant form an attitude of mind widely held among Englishmen. Of course this *obiter dictum* may have been pure cynicism, one of those judicial pleasantries which cause " laughter in court " and, out of it, amazement not at the joke but at the merriment. But if it were not that, it must, I should suppose, have meant something of this sort. The Law of God can be operative in human society only in so far as it expresses itself in positive enactments or recognised customs. These acts and customs may be either direct, the work of the supreme legislature, or they may be indirect, the acts of some other body with powers derived therefrom. The rules of the Church of England about communion were of that nature, and were abrogated by the new Act of Parliament, in spite of those words which were inserted expressly with the contrary intention. So far indeed as the words "notorious evilliver" were concerned, this contention would not be unreasonable; and it is now generally acknowledged that Canon Thompson was ill-advised in using this rubric in the earlier stages of the case as part of his justification. It may be well argued that the word "notorious" has reference, not to Church Law but to common opinion; and that no one can be said to be a notorious evilliver who does what an Act of Parliament empowers him to do. The case would not be dissimilar if the Church were disestablished; for in that case a man excommunicated under these terms would have the right to bring an action for libel, and it would be quite open for a jury to take the view that "notorious" had reference to the general morality of the country and not to the particular code of the religious body.

But the point in this case is the denial of the authority of the Canons and the abrogation of the *Table of Prohibited Degrees* by a pure Act of State. It is probable that in the case of a non-established communion this would not be attempted. Yet it is clear from the law of libel and slander that the grounds of excommunication would have to be specifically stated in the formularies, or definite power to exclude given by some clause, or else there would once more be a conflict of laws, and the sect might find itself unable to maintain its own rites of exclusion. Mere disestablishment would not of itself ensure liberty.

For this reason I do not wish to discuss the question of disestablishment. At bottom it is irrelevant to the issue. The real problem is the relation of smaller communities to that "*communitas communitatum*" we call the State, and whether they have an existence of their own or are the mere creatures of the sovereign. It might indeed be true as a matter of fact that disestablishment is the necessary condition in this country of the recognition in the Church of those principles I am trying to set down. But if so, it is mere fact; for in the case of the Established Kirk of Scotland this recognition exists to a large extent, while in certain other cases where a Church is not established it is still without real freedom.

At the same time, since the use of the term " Establishment " to denote the Church of England is largely responsible for the form, if not the matter, of our difficulties, it may be well to say a few words on the topic. The word " establish " seems to me to have changed its connotation somewhere in the course of the eighteenth century. In the apology of the Commons of 1604, after saying that they " have not come in any Puritan or Brownish spirit to introduce their parity or to work the subversion of the State ecclesiastical," they go on to say that they do not " desire so much that any man in regard of weakness of conscience may be exempted after Parliament from obedience unto *laws established* " as that new laws may be enacted.[1] Here the phrase is used evidently to denote the laws of the Elizabethan settlement. The Church of England as by law established, if such a phrase could then have been employed, would have meant not as by law founded, but as by law settled ; it refers not to the origin of the Church, but to its control.

---

[1] The document is given in Prothero's *Statutes and Constitutional Documents,* pp. 286–93.

Thus these words indicate the following things. The series of legal changes beginning in the reign of Henry VIII had practically destroyed benefit of clergy and subjected all clerks to the law of the land; the Elizabethan settlement sanctioned by the Act of Uniformity had "established," or sought to establish, one and one only form of legal service in the Church of England in contradistinction of the ancient variety of uses from diocese to diocese; while the Act of Supremacy (under the 8th clause of which the Court of High Commission was set up) and the various statutes against Roman and Jesuit propaganda had surrounded the régime with a strong police bulwark against all who strove to upset it. What the faithful Commons were thinking of was the fact of the settlement and the sanction of it in the Law of England. They had no notion of an established, as opposed to a non-established Church, for in our sense of the word the latter was a conception which had not crossed their minds, however congruous it was to that of Robert Browne in his *Reformation without Tarrying for Any*. But

after the Revolution, and still more after
the Union with Scotland in 1707, things
had changed. With the Toleration Act
came a definite legal status for religious
bodies other than the Church of England.
With the non-juring schism came the definite denial on the part of the strongest
Episcopalians of the need or importance of
establishment, while with the Union there
came the spectacle of two Churches—one
Presbyterian, one Episcopalian—equally
established in the United Kingdom. All
these considerations, aided by the growth
of voluntaryism in Scotland, led to that
distinction between established and non-
established Churches, which we think so
natural, but was inconceivable, not merely
in the Middle Ages, but through the greater
part of the seventeenth century. Instead
of talking of the Church as by law established, men began to talk of "the Established Church," and eventually, though
perhaps more in Scotland than in England,
simply of "the Establishment." The word
came to have the meaning of "privileged,"
or, officially, the State religion, as distinct
from those bodies which, though tolerated

and in one sense established (as Lord Mans-
field said), were private in their nature,
partaking of no official or national character.
After this it was easy for the unhistori-
cally minded to achieve the view that the
Church was an institution founded and supported by the State for its own purposes,
with no powers of any kind except as delegated by Parliament.   This notion was
stimulated by the Roman Catholic claim
that the events of the sixteenth century
were in no sense a development, but the
substitution of a body entirely new ; while,
on the other hand, the Puritan dislike of
the whole Catholic system had led to the
entrenchment within the Church of England
of a strong body of opinion equally anxious to
confine the Church within the four corners of
sixteenth-century Protestantism.   All this
has been strengthened by the growth of
parliamentary sovereignty and what Professor Dicey in his *Law of the Constitution*
has taught us to call the "rule of law."
The extent to which Parliament has ab-
sorbed into itself every kind of jurisdiction,
and the modern growth of State action,
together with that legal prejudice we shall

have soon to consider, have all contributed
to produce a state of things in which, for
a large majority of people, not only are
there no inherent rights in the Established
Church, but there are none in any religious
body, none in any secular society, not even
the family; while for many more any notion
of a rule of morality, as distinct from a rule
of law, seems almost blasphemy. A capital
instance is the attitude of the jurists towards
International Law. International Law, as
is well known, cannot be brought under the
Austinian rubric, because by the very nature
of the case it is imposed by no determinate
sovereign. In consequence of that there
has prevailed among many jurists (as distinct from publicists) a sort of prejudice
against it, as though because it had no irresistible sanctions it not only was not law,
but was not even custom; and further, as
though short of a physical sanction it was
not even desirable that public opinion should
be stimulated to the point of demanding
that international relations should be conducted in accordance with any rules of
action save immediate convenience. In
other words, this exaltation of the Austinian

sovereign has led to the depreciation not
only of religion and morality, but of all State
action save that of the purest Machiavel-
lianism, and would, if logically employed,
have justified the worst excesses of bar-
barism.   As a matter of fact, I believe
this conception of law to be no more than
verbally justifiable, and to be practically
dangerous.   But that I shall try to show
later on.   At present we are concerned
with the question of fact—the denial to
the Church of any real inherent life.   Let
me quote what Professor Dicey says in his
Law and Public Opinion.   The Divorce
Act of 1857 has commonly been regarded
as a great invasion of the rights of the
Church, in that it compels the incumbent, not indeed to marry, but to allow
the use of his church for the marriage of
divorced persons.   Mr. Dicey, however,
writes as follows of even that narrow ex-
emption allowed by the Act: " A clergyman of the Church of England is, after all,
an official of the national Church; but
under the Divorce Act he is allowed to
decline to solemnise the marriage of any
person whose former marriage has been dis-

solved on the ground of his or her adultery. Thus a clergyman, while acting as an official of the State, is virtually allowed to pronounce immoral a marriage permitted by the morality of the State." [1]

That is the view, then, of this eminent authority, who represents, I should suppose, better than almost any man the average opinion of the highly trained jurist, and is our highest living expert in Constitutional Law. He dislikes the mere minimum of liberty allowed in the Act of 1857 (which Mr. Gladstone never ceased to oppose as being contrary to the liberty of the Church), and regards this grudging permission as a dangerous concession to a non-national power. It is clear that the writer deprecates the notion that the Christian Church can have a higher law than that of the State; indeed he would appear to go farther and to identify legal with moral right. Although this is not definitely stated to be the author's view, yet it seems to be his feeling, that ethics no less than religion is the creature of the State. It may be urged that this attitude is a consequence

[1] *Law and Public Opinion*, p. 315.

only of establishment, and that if the Church were disestablished it would cease from the legal standpoint to be national, and that its inherent spiritual authority would at once be recognised. Is this certain? That some change in this direction would follow is probable, but it does not necessarily result from the fact of disestablishment, and with juristic notions being what they are such freedom would probably fall very short of anything desired. We have in this matter one or two instances before our eyes. Let us see what light they throw on the problem.

No one will claim for the Roman Church that she is in the United Kingdom an established body in the technical sense. Certainly it might have been thought she would make rules for her own members, and in many respects she does so. The recent discussions about the *ne temere* decree have enlightened us. Had it been claimed that that decree should have any bearing on the question of legal marriage it would indeed be an invasion of the sphere of the civil power. But not content with affirming this undoubted fact, many have gone further. One Member of Parliament, who represents a great University, is reported to have " denied that it was in the power or right of any Church to superadd its own conditions on what the law considered to be sufficient in the case of civil marriage." [1] It may be said that this is an isolated opinion, that it represents neither the policy of the Government nor the practice of the Courts. But it is fair evidence of the state of mind of many Englishmen, and its logical results can only be termed preposterous. If *per impossibile* the suggestions of that brilliant dramatist who teaches morality to the modern world were to be fulfilled, and divorce were to be made " as cheap, as easy, and as secret as possible," this principle would make it impossible for

---

[1] " Even if this decree in its operation had been confined to the members of the Roman Catholic religion in Ireland, I should have bitterly resented it, because I 'don't think it is in the power or duty or right of any Church to superadd its own conditions to what the law considers to be sufficient in the case of civil marriage." It is clear that on this principle the Christian Church in its early development was acting wrongly in establishing for its own members a higher standard of morality than that of the Pagan world.—*Parliamentary Debates*, Feb. 7, 1911, col. 151.

B

any religious body to maintain itself against the promiscuous adultery which it would render possible.   Moreover, the attack on monogamous marriage as a lifelong institution is now so universal and important, that at any moment measures might be proposed which not the wildest imagination would call Christian.[1]

Marriage, however, though it is the storm-centre, is by no means the only matter on which we can detect this reluctance on the part of statesmen and lawyers to allow religious bodies to develop according to their own inherent spirit—and not merely by an externally imposed rule.   An object-lesson of value is the famous case of the *Free Church of Scotland Appeals*.   This we can read at length in Mr. Orr's reprint of the official report.   You remember the facts.   A strong party in the great Free Kirk which had issued from the Disruption of 1843 had laboured under the leadership of Principal Rainy to promote union with

[1] *Cf.* Ellen Key, *Love and Marriage*, especially chap. viii., "Free Divorce"; and *The Truth about Woman*, C. Gascoigne Hartley.   These two works alone will show the reader what open attacks are being made on every element of morality.

the older body, the United Presbyterians.
This union which was ultimately effected
was resisted by a small body known as the
" Wee Frees," who declared the amalgama-
tion to be *ultra vires*. The most important
of the contentions on their side were as
follows. It was asserted that a looser interpretation was being given to the formularies,
and that to desert the rigid Calvinistic doctrine was so far destroying the foundations,
that the identity of the Free Kirk in the
new United Free would not be maintained.
Secondly, it was alleged that Chalmers and
his party, while objecting to certain abuses
in the Established Kirk, had also declared themselves in favour of the principle of Establishment, and that this was
now abandoned through the union with the
United Presbyterians, a body pledged to
voluntaryism. These contentions were held
to be made good by the House of Lords,
to which the case was eventually carried.
In other words, the Act by which the union
had been carried was condemned as *ultra
vires*, and all the property of the Free Kirk
was adjudged to belong to the small community (or Wee Frees) who held to the

original notions.   The decision seemed absurd enough from the practical standpoint, but its results in Scotland would have been tragic had the judgment been carried out.   So widespread was the discontent that an Act of Parliament was at once passed, setting up a body of commissioners with power to apportion the property in such proportions as might be deemed equitable between the two sections of the original Free Kirk, and without regard to the recent decision.   This, however, does not alter the fact that the judgment of the House of Lords expressed the mind of English lawyers on a topic of such importance, and shows us how they would regard all claims to independent life on the part of a religious body.   Since these bodies were " Free Churches " the question was not complicated by any specifically limiting consequences of State establishment.   The problem came up in a more universal form, and the decision should serve as a warning to those who think that disestablishment of itself would save all risk of inconvenient action on the part of the State.   How far the " claim of right "

originally put forward may have affected
the issue we need not here inquire. What
is certain is, that the Lords (with the exception of Lord Macnaghten[1] and Lord
Lindley) found themselves unable to conceive the notion of a Church, refusing at
any moment to consider more than the
terms of the trust. Tacitly, if not explicitly, they denied any real and inherent
power of development; and further, so
far from refusing to consider theological

---

[1] Some of Lord Macnaghten's phrases are worthy of
citation here. "The question, therefore, seems to me
to be this: Was the Church thus purified—the Free
Church—so bound and tied by the tenets of the Church
of Scotland prevailing at the time of Disruption, that
departure from these tenets in any matter of substance
would be a violation of that profession or testimony
which may be called the unwritten charter of her
foundation, and so necessarily involve a breach of trust
in the administration of funds contributed for no other
purpose but the support of the Free Church—the
Church of the Disruption? Was the Free Church by
the very condition of her existence forced to cling
to her Subordinate Standards with so desperate a grip
that she has lost hold and touch of the Supreme
Standard of her faith? Was she from birth incapable
of all growth and development? Was she (in a word)
a dead branch, and not a living Church?"—Orr, *Free
Church of Scotland Appeals*, p. 573.

questions, they listened to a long argument of Mr. [now Lord] Haldane designed to show that from the higher Hegelian standpoint Calvinism and Arminianism were really the same thing.   This the Lords were forced to do in order to judge whether or no the new Act contravened the original trust.   Thus on the one hand the judgment denies to a Free Church the power of defining and developing in its own doctrine; and on the other, while disclaiming interference in theological matters, it practically exercises it under the plea of considering the question whether or no the trust had been violated.   If the real life of the religious body had been admitted, the question as to whether or no the new theology of the united body was in agreement with that of the old Free Kirk would have become one of fact, not of law, and in that case the overwhelming majority in favour of the union would probably have been sufficient evidence.[1]   But this view was not taken.

[1] *Mr. Haldane*—"Well, my Lord, my argument at your Lordship's bar is this, that if you ask, what is the test of identity, the test of the personal identity

Other instances yet more pertinent to the general topic, though of less dangerous import for Englishmen, may be cited from more than one Continental State. In the two cases of the Law of the Associations and that of Separation in France, we have

of this Church lies, not in doctrine, but in its life, in the continuity of its life, as ascertained by the fact that the majority have continuously kept on doing these things, which are within their competence according to our opinion."—Orr, p. 518.

Again, with reference to the claim to relax the terms of subscription, Lord Macnaghten goes on : " If the Church has power to release the stringency of the formulæ required from her ministers and office-bearers, so as to avoid offence to the consciences of the most conscientious and to keep within her fold the most able and enlightened of her probationers, that is all that is required. That she has that power I cannot doubt. These formulæ were imposed by Act of Parliament. If they owe their force and efficiency in the Established Church to Acts of Parliament, the Free Church has rejected the ordinances of men and the authority of Parliament, and is free to regulate her own formulæ. If in the Established Church they owe this force wholly or in part to the antecedent recognition of the Church, the Free Church, as it seems to me, claiming to act and recognised by her adherents as acting in the character of a national Church, and proceeding regularly in accordance with the constitution of the Church, may do now what the Church did in the seventeenth century."—*Ibid.*, p. 576.

instances of State tyranny which "jump
to the eyes." Under the former the property of the English Benedictines was
confiscated, although they had settled in
France for a perfectly lawful purpose and
on the faith of State protection. It was
made criminal for men or women to live
together in a common life without special
leave obtained from the Government; and,
as we know now, contrary to the intention of
the original proposer, that leave was withheld in almost every case from religious
communities, although I think that some
exceptions were made for nursing sisters.
If anyone doubts that persecution of the
most definite kind was practised and intended, I would suggest that he should
peruse the speeches made in defence of the
application of the law by the French
Prime Minister, M. Emile Combes. They
are published under the title *Une Campagne
Laïque*, prefaced by a diatribe from M.
Anatole France. True, the persecution was
not of religious convictions or practices
as such, but of all associations to develop
religion in a communal life, on the ground,
nominally, that such unions were inimical

to the omnipotence of the State. It was more than the assertion of the theory (which I shall try later to explain), known as the concession theory of corporate life, in an extreme form; for it not only denied these bodies the legal position of corporate personalities, but it denied to the individuals composing them the right to live together—and as a fact dissolved and dispersed the monastic houses. Similar instances of State interference can be found in the details of the Law of Separation; although not in the principle of dissolving the *concordat* and setting the Church and the State apart.[1] The new law, so far from recognising the rights of French Catholics to their own ecclesiastical polity, to say the least leaves it doubtful. The property of

[1] The text both of the Associations Law of 1901 and the Separation Law of 1905 will be found in the Appendix to Mr. J. E. C. Bodley's two lectures on "The Church in France." His remarks at the beginning of Lecture II on the attitude of Frenchmen towards the principle of association are valuable. Only I would suggest that the dislike which he speaks of is not merely the product of the individualism of the French Revolution, but goes right back to the genesis of the Latin world, of Roman Law, and the Emperor Trajan.

each parish was to be vested in an *associa-tion cultuelle;* but there was no guarantee in these associations for that episcopal government alone recognised by Catholics.[1] There was nothing to prevent a small body of malcontents getting hold of the machine and ousting the bishop from all power. It is persistently argued that the Pope was ill-advised in repudiating the concessions of the Government and refusing to allow the French Catholics to accept these *associations cultuelles.* I do not presume to say whether or no the universal outcry against the alleged short-sightedness of Cardinal Merry del Val was justified. For it may be that in this, as in other instances, it might have been wise for the sake of the benefits to admit the invasion of rights; and so long as the loyalty of the Catholics was assured, the associations might have worked well

---

[1] It is a question how far the qualifying words in Art. 4, *en se conformant aux règles d'organisation générale du culte dont elles se proposent d'assurer l'exercice,* really would ensure the episcopal government; for Clause 8 contemplates two rival associations, and grants the decision to the Council of State. At any rate, it is always claimed on the Roman Catholic side that the law does not give adequate security.

enough. But I am certain that on grounds
of theory the action of the Pope was clearly
justified, provided he was right in the facts:
" So long as it should not be legally and
certainly evident, that the Divine Constitution of the Church, the immutable rights
of the Roman Pontiff and of the bishop,
such as their authority over the necessary
property of the Church, particularly the
sacred edifices, would in the said associations
be irrevocably and fully secure." That is, it
denies such right so far as questions of the
property in churches are concerned; while I
think it is not allowed to build other churches.
But this is not all. Since the Pope refused
to accept the Law of Separation, the property
is actually vested in the Communes. These
local authorities are bound not to interfere
with the religious worship, and also to keep
them in repair. In the event of any build-
ing being in such disrepair that it is unfit
for use, they may close it. In some dis-
tricts where the local authorities are anti-
Christian, this is the course they are taking.
Unable by law to close the churches for
worship, they are refusing to repair them,
refusing also to allow the Catholics to repair

them at their own expense, while no other churches can be built without their leave. In a few years' time they will be able to order the churches to be closed on the ground that they are no longer fit for use. This policy is, of course, not universal; it is said to be only applied to buildings of no architectural merit, and it would, I suppose, be difficult to prove against the Government as a whole.   But it is only a further instance of the definitely persecuting spirit of the French Positivists, which indeed goes a great deal further than the actual law. During the debates on the law one deputy openly demanded that public worship should be prohibited in the cathedrals; and another utterance is often quoted, " We have extinguished in heaven those lights which men shall never light again."   All this and further facts seem to me clear evidence of a definitely organised and strongly supported attempt to set up a Positivist Church State, and to maintain it by persecution.   This position was really contemplated by Comte, and awakened thereby the abhorrence of Mill, who on other grounds admired his system.   It is tacitly admitted by M. Emile

Combes, and can be seen also at work in Portugal. Such dangers may seem remote in this country, and its real hold on religion is doubtless far stronger. But these facts serve to show the absurdity of the notion that the persecuting spirit is confined to believers in religion; while some arise definitely from the dogma of the omnipotence of the State.

Another instance even more notable was the *Kultur-kampf*. This is more striking, because it is a case in which the strongest nineteenth-century statesman met more than his match. It is also more pertinent to England, because it was concerned not with an attempt to destroy Christianity, but rather with an attempt to maintain one particular form of it, and that the form with which many of us here would most sympathise. Prince Bismarck, though himself a Protestant, thought that he saw in the old Catholic movement a hopeful opportunity of finally destroying the power of Rome in Germany. The Lutheran revolution was only partial, and there never was any prospect after the sixteenth century of its winning the Catholic States. But now, owing to the relative novelty of the doctrine of Papal infallibility, and the fact that some of the most learned and influential of the German-speaking Catholics, *e.g.* Döllinger and Strossmayer, had opposed the definition, there seemed a fair chance of throwing off the last fetters of Roman authority. The old Catholic movement, if sufficiently supported by the Government, might absorb all the Catholic elements, and a new Church, if not Lutheran, at least not Roman and entirely the instrument of the State, would result.

The conflict spread far. The famous Falk or Mai Laws were passed to ensure the victory of the Government; bishops and others were imprisoned for long periods. But all in vain. Although the doctrine of State omnipotence was proclaimed in terms that might have satisfied Machiavelli, the convictions of German Catholics and their loyalty to Rome were proof against all persecution; and in spite of saying " We will not go to Canossa," Prince Bismarck was eventually forced to capitulate, and the Roman Church won an unqualified triumph. The details of the conflict do not concern us. But its principles do. For it was in the most naked form a struggle between the believers in the doctrine of State absolutism and those who held by the right of a religious society to form its own rules and to direct its own members. The fact that our own sympathies may be in most respects with the Old Catholics (as against the preposterous Papal absolutism) should in no way blind us to the real issue between Bismarck and his opponents. Indeed no one who believes in liberty of conscience can do other than rejoice at the most astounding catastrophe in the career of that ever-victorious statesman. I would recommend that you should consult in this subject Nielsen's *History of the Papacy in the Nineteenth Century.* Bishop Nielsen's standpoint is very far from being Roman Catholic, but he makes it quite clear to any reader that the action of the Prussian Government was unjustifiable and in the strictest sense a religious persecution.

I mention these Continental cases because they all help to show that the doctrine against which we are bound to struggle is no special prejudice of the English mind,

but that it is a part of the common heritage
of Europe, and is indeed probably more
acutely defined in these countries where
the Roman Civil Law has been for centuries " received." Just as the right of
the religious society to be and to develop
its own inherent life is an elementary right
common to all political society, so the claim
of the State to an uncontrolled and ultimately to an arbitrary authority is a universal claim, and is not merely the product
of our peculiar conditions or of the establishment and endowment of the Church of
England. At the same time it may be
more convenient to consider the topic
mainly from the standpoint of Englishmen,
or at least of that of citizens of the United
Kingdom.

Let us return then to the case of the
Scotch Churches. Does it not seem as
though there must be something fundamentally erroneous in a decision which
proved so practically unworkable as that
of the House of Lords? The judgment, it
is said, could have been executed only at the
cost of something like civil war, and did as
a matter of fact produce rioting in several

places before the settlement was made which abrogated it. Apart from any special or technical points, what we find in this case is that the lawyers refused to consider the body as a Church, *i.e.* as a society with a principle of inherent life, but bound it rigidly by the dead hand of its original documents. They construed it as a mechanism, not as an organic life. The actual decision could only be paralleled if an English Court had chosen to adjudge all the property of the English Roman Catholics to someone who had refused to submit to the Vatican decrees on the ground that they were *ultra vires*, and if the judgment had been given after a discussion in court of the meaning of the creed of Pope Pius V. For, as we saw, despite their protestations to the contrary, we find the judges driven to discuss those very theological topics for which they confessed themselves to be unfitted. Since they refused to recognise the society as such, but would only consider the trusts, they were unable to treat these questions as matters of fact and take the opinion of the officers of the Church as to whether or no they were *ultra vires*. They were forced in spite of

themselves to go into the question of the
terms of the trust while all the while pro-
fessedly neutral. Thus we have the serio-
comic spectacle of Lord Haldane, the
translator of Schopenhauer, with his acute
metaphysical genius, nourished on Hegel's
Encyklopädie, endeavouring to place the
results of his meditations on the true meaning of the Westminster Confession before
the characteristically Anglo-Saxon mentality of Lord Halsbury and Lord James
of Hereford. Let me read you one or two
passages :

Mr. Haldane—Your Lordship is assuming, if I may respectfully say so, an anthropo-
morphic conception of the Supreme Being.
It is very difficult to discuss these things,
but I must say your Lordship is really
assuming that the Supreme Being stands to
a particular man in the relation of another
man—a cause external to Him in space and
time acting in space and time, and separate
from Him as one thing is separate from
another. The whole point of the specu-
lative teaching has been that this is not so ;
the whole point of the Church has been
that that is a totally inadequate conception,

and that at any rate, without resorting to any explanation, they have to hold the two things as in harmony and reconcilable.

Lord James of Hereford—Mr. Haldane, till you told me so I had not the slightest idea that I was conceiving that.

Mr. Haldane—I am afraid, my Lord, theologians would deal severely with your Lordship's statement.

Lord James of Hereford—I am much obliged to you.[1]

When we find English secular lawyers in the twentieth century endeavouring to decide between legitimate and illegitimate "developments" of the Westminster Confession, we feel ourselves almost like Alice in Wonderland. Only it is the wonderland of fact—that strangest of all realities, the legal mind.[2]

[1] Orr, p. 504.

[2] The Church is like an organism; the materials may change, and there may be metabolism of every item of which it consists, and yet the Church goes on preserving its organic life through the medium of its system of Church government, which provides for a Supreme Assembly, supreme in that matter of doctrine to which your Lordship referred, and which I agree was a distinctive matter of doctrine at the time the Church was founded.—Orr, p. 479.

If we try to get behind the judgment to the minds of the judges and the conception of law which dominates them, I think it will be found that its failure to harmonise the facts lies above all in this—that in their view the Church did not exist at all, *i.e.* the Church as a living social union of men bound together by specific ties, recruited by definite means, and acting by virtue of an inherent spontaneity of life which is not imposed but original, which though it may be regulated by the civil authority is not derived therefrom.   That that was the conception of the Kirk in the mind of Chalmers is unquestionable: it is indeed the very irony of fate that a body formed for no other purpose but to maintain a passionate sense of corporate freedom should be declared by the Courts of Law to be lacking in that very quality of spontaneous life which the fathers of the Disruption had gone into the wilderness to assert.[1]   Now

[1] Every point they have been contending here, if raised immediately the day after the Disruption, would have stultified what those who brought about the Disruption had done.—Orr, p. 479.

Again, My Lords, that is the very point upon which the Disruption took place, and I do not see myself how

this conception is not merely the claim of
the Scots Free Kirk; it is the notion of
every religious sect which claims for itself
toleration. None can really admit that its
entity is derived from the State. It is the
boast of the Free Churches in this country

my learned friends could have maintained their contention at the Bar without being in the view of the
Free Church at that time incapable of being received
into its membership on the ground that they were
setting up that very interference of the Civil Courts in
spiritual matters which the Free Church had broken off
from the State in order to assert in the most unqualified
form.—Orr, p. 492. [The word "assert" is surely
wrong here, unless a clause such as "freedom from
which" be understood after "spiritual matters."]

One cannot conceive that the Free Church meant
when it came out that their synods were to be
at the call of the Civil Magistrate. That would be
totally inconsistent with the very conception of their
Church. Their synods were to be called by themselves; Christ is the only Head. To be at the call of
the Civil Magistrate would be totally inconsistent with
that conception. What I mean is, they did in 1846
exactly what they do now. They proceeded to interpret the Confession of Faith in a way which, in my
view of it, amounted to a modification. They did it in
1846, and, if my friend's argument is right, they did it
at the risk of an interdict which could have been
obtained the next day from the Court of Session to
restrain them from so doing. The relevancy of that

that they have secured the recognition of this right, while we are debarred from it, and in their view justly debarred, by the accident of establishment. But this case argument is this. There are two conceptions of this case ; *one is that in* 1846 *what really happened was that a sum of money was gathered together and put upon certain trusts to preach a certain doctrine*—the doctrine which is contained in the Confession and other doctrines. The other view is this, that the first thing they did when they came out, as a result of their controversy, was to establish a Church, and then a subsequent step was to gather together the property for the use of that Church, and to put it at the disposal of the Church. —Orr, p. 528.

Again (p. 531) : It was the element of the Church to determine the question of doctrine, and the Civil Court, which had the civil authority, was *bound to accept the interpretation* which the contract assigns to the Church exclusively.

Suppose somebody in 1846 had said : " No, you had no business to put in these words about persecuting principles," can it be for a moment supposed that the Free Church would have considered that the Court was intended by their constitution to have had jurisdiction to discuss that question ? They would have said : " No ; the very thing for which we came out was to get independence of the decision of this Court on this question of doctrine, and, so far as property comes in, our property was accumulated after we had become a Church, and was intended to be held at the disposition of the Church, constituted with these powers of legislative independence " (p. 534).

shows how illusory is this notion. I think indeed that we must admit that no established Church can claim quite the same liberty as one non-established. But my point is that in the existing state of the law there is no security that either the one or the other will really be allowed this liberty when it comes to the pinch. I think we must agree that our Church, so long as she is established, cannot in reason claim the whole of the halfpence ; that to demand an entire independence of the State while enjoying peculiar privileges is neither right nor prudent. Yet, on the other hand, neither should it get all the kicks, as the poor Church of England seems like to do in the present state of the public mind.

What really concerns us is not so much whether or no a religious body be in the technical sense established, but whether or no it be conceived as possessing any living power of self-development, or whether it is conceived either as a creature of the State, or if allowed a private title is to be held rigidly under the trust-deeds of her foundation, thereby enslaved to the dead. Not indeed that all change should be taken as admissible, but that those changes sanctioned (as was this) by the constitutional authority of the Church, and declared by them to be in accordance with the spirit of their society, should be accepted as such by the courts, and no further question asked. In other words, is the life of the society to be conceived as inherent or derived ? Does the Church exist by some inward living force, with powers of self-development like a person ; or is she a mere aggregate, a fortuitous concourse of ecclesiastical atoms, treated it may be as one for purposes of convenience, but with no real claim to a mind or will of her own, except so far as the civil power sees good to invest her for the nonce with a fiction of unity ?

Since, as a fact, religious bodies are only one class of a number of other societies, all laying claim to this inherent life, it is clear that the question concerns not merely ecclesiastical privilege, but the whole complex structure of civil society and the nature of political union. It cannot be too often repeated, that the primary question at issue is no narrow quibble of a few bigoted clergy and ecclesiastically-minded laymen,

but has to do with the quality of all persons
other than natural persons in the nation.[1]
Are corporate societies to be conceived as
real personalities or as fictitious ones, *i.e.* is
their union to be throughout of such a
nature that it has a life greater than the
mere sum of the individuals composing the
body; that it is not merely a matter of
contract; that in action it has the marks of
mind and will which we attribute to personality; that this corporate life and personality
grows up naturally and inevitably out of
any union of men for permanent ends, and
is not withheld or granted at the pleasure
of the State? Of course the State may
and must require certain marks, such as
proofs of registration, permanence, constitution, before it recognises the personality
of societies, just as it does, though in a less
degree, in the case of individuals; and the
complex nature of the body may necessitate
a more complex procedure. Also the State

---

[1] *Cf.* Gierke, *Das Wesen des Menschlichen Verbände*,
p. 10: "Sind vielleicht die menschlichen Verbände
reale Einheiten, die mit der Anerkennung ihrer Persönlichkeit durch das Recht nur das empfangen, was ihrer
wirklichen Beschaffenheit entspricht?"

will have to regulate and control the
relations of corporate persons to one another
and to natural persons. But all this does
not and need not imply that corporate
personality is the gift of the sovereign, a
mere name to be granted or withheld at its
pleasure ; and that permanent societies can
come into being and go on acting without
it.   It is, in a word, a real life and personality which those bodies are forced to claim,
which we believe that they possess by the
nature of the case, and not by the arbitrary
grant of the sovereign.   To deny this real
life is to be false to the facts of social
existence, and is of the same nature as that
denial of human personality which we call
slavery, and is always in its nature unjust
and tyrannical.

Yet this denial is the notion dominant
to-day in modern Europe, and is the presupposition of the average legal arrangements, although it is beginning to decay.
Into the origin of this claim to State
absolutism, with its attendant denial of all
corporate existence other than fictitious, we
shall inquire next time.   But what I want
to make clear to-day is, that this notion is

well-nigh universal, that it is precisely one
which no religious society can admit without being false to the very idea of its
existence, or placing the Divine Law at the
mercy of political convenience.

From these instances which I have
named (and others are probably familiar
to you) it seems clear that the moment
the religious body begins to act as though
it had any inherent life, it is liable to be
hauled up in the courts and to be condemned as having acted *ultra vires*. In
the case of our own Church, there are many
further evidences of the disinclination of
average opinion to admit that the Church
has any real social entity or any standard
either of doctrine or discipline, except that
of the nation at large. Recent discussions
illustrate this. The action of the Bishop
of Hereford in publicly inviting Dissenters
to receive the Holy Communion has been
the occasion of a widespread debate on the
Confirmation Test. Whether or no there
may not be something to be said for such
a dispensation from the rubric on a great
national occasion, I shall not inquire. But
what has been noteworthy throughout the

discussion is this. At bottom there lay the claim, that there ought to be no rules at all about communion; that every Englishman who desired had a right to partake of our altars; and that for the religious society to claim any powers of exclusion is preposterous.

Similar claims have been put forward in doctrinal matters. A certain book[1] has raised acutely the question of the ethics of conformity. The question was not merely argued, as it might have been, on the ground that the particular claims put forward were allowable, or that the individual miracles were only accidental. On the contrary, a further claim was put forward to an entire freedom in historical criticism, which is logically destructive of any claim of Christianity to be an historical religion. If the principles put forward were carried out there would not be the smallest ground for objecting to a .clergyman disbelieving not only the miraculous but all the other elements in the Gospel narrative; and we

[1] *Miracles in the New Testament*, by Rev. J. M. Thompson. I speak here of the defenders, not the writer of this work.

might hope to see followers of Professor Drews one day seated in the chair of St. Augustine. Nor indeed could this freedom once granted be confined to historical criticism; it would have to be extended to ethical and philosophical topics. The same liberty could justly be claimed for some followers of Nietzsche, who believe that the upward development of humanity can only come from the destruction of Christian ethics; or from some disciple of Comte, who desired a system ethically Christian but entirely bounded by this world.

The hopeless confusion of thought between the right of the individual to choose for himself and his right to remain in a society pledged to one thing while he himself is pledged to the opposite would be incredible were it not so widespread, and would be the death-blow of all the political clubs that ever existed. No one would claim the right of being president of a Tariff Reform club, while desiring to propagate Free Trade. Yet precisely the same is claimed, at least by implication, in all these discussions about free criticism. The ground of this confusion is the absolute lack of any sense that the Church has a reality and life of her own; that she means something. Otherwise claims so preposterous would not be thought of.

Somewhat similar objections lie at the bottom of the dislike of denominational education. Only here the objection comes not so much from failure to perceive the fact as from the acute perception of it, combined with equally acute dislike. The speeches of Dr. Clifford have all along been perfectly consistent and, from his standpoint, justifiable. They are the clearest expressions of a view which is dominant in the greater part of the undenominationalist camp. What Dr. Clifford dislikes is the fact that denominationalism means the recognition of the religious society as such in the matter of education; what he demands is that there shall be no intermediary between the State and the child. Passionate as he is in his expression, his meaning is always clear; the claims alike of the religious body and of the family are to be set aside or rather denied; and the child (if he be come of poor parents) is to be treated in this matter as belonging to the

State alone. No other society is to be tolerated; and therefore the "right of entry" of its officers, *i.e.* the priest, is to be withheld, and all distinctively denominational education is to be abolished. It is all lucid, logical, and deliberate; and it springs quite naturally from that passion for State absolutism which is the child of the Renaissance and Reform and the grandchild of the Pagan State.

Now the State did not create the family, nor did it create the Churches; nor even in any real sense can it be said to have created the club or the trades union; nor in the Middle Ages the guild or the religious order, hardly even the universities or the colleges within the universities: they have all arisen out of the natural associative instincts of mankind, and should all be treated by the supreme authority as having a life original and guaranteed, to be controlled and directed like persons, but not regarded in their corporate capacity as mere names, which for juristic purposes and for these purposes only are entitled persons. As a matter of fact, in England at least, it is these smaller associations which have always counted for most in the life of the individual. His school or college, his parish or county, his union or regiment, his wife or family is the most vitally formative part in the life of most men ; and in so far as England has anything worthy in civic life to show to the world, it is the spectacle of individuals bred up or living within these small associations which mould the life of men more intimately than does the great collectivity we call the State. Nor are they mere slices of government departments, but in fact, if not in theory, are infinitely diverse, and even where pledged to the same ends has each its own individuality, its own ἦθος, which breathe a spirit not of to-day nor yesterday, but of the long line of famous men who have shared in this common life and handed down enriched the treasure of a great and living tradition. Which of us has not been thrilled by that wonderful commemoration lesson, " Let us now praise famous men and our fathers that begat us " ? Which of us is not moved by loyalty and an affection that seems independent of circumstances to one or other of these venerable institutions which, so far from hindering, fosters and develops his loyalty to the great "society of societies" we call the State; and which of us would not be more than scandalised to be told that this common life had no reality at all or meaning, but that it was merely the contractual union of a number of individuals, whose individuality was in no way changed by these social bonds, and were each of them purely independent and atomic—so that social life is like a heap of sand, rather than a living being? And yet this is the inevitable and logical consequence, if not in practice at least in theory, of that doctrine of the State in its relation to smaller societies which is not merely prevalent as an opinion, but is the only doctrine even conceivable in the mind of the average lawyer.

What I have tried in this lecture to make clear is this: that we are divided from our adversaries by questions of principle, not of detail; that the principle is concerned not with the details of ecclesiastical privilege or with the special position of an Established Church, but with the very nature of the corporate life of men, and

D

therefore with the true nature of the State; that the very least we can claim as a religious body is more than will be admitted by the other side; for it is most true, as I once heard an eminent mathematician declare, that "the English people have not yet realised the idea of a Church." At the same time there is hope; not only are the clouds of prejudice around us dissolving, and the greatest of historical jurists, Gierke, Maitland, and others, inculcating a more real view of the nature of the corporate life; but from many sides and causes influences are tending to help us in our struggle, if we will only use them rightly. In Church matters, now that the conflict is passing from one on matters of ritual to questions which concern the deepest facts of social life, we shall have many willing to make common cause with us who previously were disposed to be contemptuous of what appeared a mere partisan conflict. Such cases as I have cited are serving to indicate that free Churches are not so free as they supposed, so long as this doctrine of State omnipotence remains unconquered, and we may find supporters where we least expect it; while other matters of social and economic importance are clearly involved which will serve to show that in fighting their own battles religious bodies are fighting the battle of a healthy national life and alone providing the framework under which the perennial social instincts of men can develop, and instead of a scientific monstrosity (that of the omnipotent State facing an equally unreal aggregate of unrelated individuals) we may look for a land covered with every kind of social life, functioning not only in matters religious, intellectual, artistic, but also in the most necessary form of industrial and manufacturing and even agricultural activity, and each receiving its due place as a living member of the body politic, recognised as a real self-developing unity. It is because the ground on which we stand is nothing narrow or mean, but is the only security for true social liberty, and is eminently congruous with English life, that I am persuaded, that however long or bitter is the conflict, victory in the long run is certain. Liberty in England is a far more popular cry than equality, and it is with liberty that we are concerned. More and more is it clear that the mere individual's freedom against an omnipotent State may be no better than slavery; more and more is it evident that the real question of freedom in our day is the freedom of smaller unions to live within the whole. More and more must we have on our side all who are not dazzled by the cry of efficiency or sunk into that un-Christian materialism which has been the consequence in the more comfortable classes of the long security of England and her vast wealth. Freedom, if rightly pursued, is no petty nor merely clerical ideal; it is the noblest of all the watchwords that appeal to man, because in the last resort it always means that man is a spiritual being. However unfashionable this ideal has grown in our generation, pushed out on the one hand by the passion for getting, on the other by the abject need of better economic conditions, it never can permanently disappear, and we may say to our opponents, in the words of a famous speech: " Those great forces which the tumult of our debates may not for one moment impede or disturb; those great forces are against you; they are marshalled on our side ; and the banner which we now carry in this fight, though it may for a moment droop, yet it will still once more float aloft in the eye of heaven, and carry us, if not to an easy, at least to a certain and a not distant victory."

LECTURE II

THE GREAT LEVIATHAN

WE have seen that the refusal of many
lawyers to recognise in Churches, as such,
any real rights of life and development is
widespread and inveterate; that it cannot
be attributed merely to anti-clerical prejudice, strong though that has always been
in the profession, for it is based on principles
which must also deny the similar right to
other non-religious societies. We have seen
also that it is not specially English, but
European, and that it is of the nature rather
of an unconscious presupposition than a
mere theory. For those holding the current view seem almost unable to conceive
what Churchmen mean by claiming any
freedom for religious bodies. Thus it would
appear that the causes of this antipathy are
not new, and that we must seek for the historical origin of this prejudice far back in

history. It will be the purpose of this lecture to try and show how it arose, and to urge that it relates originally to a condition long since passed away, and that we ought to demand a view of politics which has more vital relation to the facts, instead of what is little more than an abstract theory deduced from the notion of unity. In this lecture, and indeed in the whole course, I cannot overestimate my debt to that great monument, both of erudition and profound thought, the *Das Deutsche Genossenschafts-recht* of Dr. Otto Gierke. A very small portion, by no means the most valuable, was translated by Maitland, and his Introduction forms an almost indispensable preliminary to this study. But it is greatly to be wished that sombody would translate the whole of Gierke's three volumes, or at least the last. Another work of Dr. Gierke, *Die Genossenschafts Theorie*, is less well known in England, but it is worth studying. There it is attempted to show how under the facts of modern life the civilian theory of corporations is breaking down on all hands, and that even in Germany, in spite of the deliberate adoption of the Romanist doctrine, the courts and sometimes even the laws are being constantly driven to treat corporate societies as though they were real and not fictitious persons, and to regard such personality as the natural consequence of permanent association, not a mere mark to be imposed or withheld by the sovereign power. The value of all these books is the greater for our purpose that they are in no sense ecclesiastical in tone, and that the English introduction was the work of one who described himself as a "dissenter from all the Churches." More directly concerned with ecclesiastical liberty, but at the same time universal in application, are some of the essays by Acton in the volume on " Freedom."

That the problem is really concerned with the liberty alike of the individual and of the corporate society, is best proved by such words as those of M. Emile Combes : " There are, there can be no rights except the right of the State, and there are, and there can be no other authority than the authority of the Republic." [1]   Nowhere, perhaps, has

[1] This was stated in an article in *The Independent Review*, September 1905.

the creed of materialist politics been expressed with such naked cynicism. Such a doctrine, if accepted, strikes at the roots of all higher morality and all religious freedom. It is the denial at once of the fact of conscience, the institutions of religion and the reality of the family. That this is the direction in which the forces represented by M. Combes would wish to drive Europe is clear from many circumstances. And though for the nonce this orgy of State absolutism may be restrained by certain surviving institutions of freedom and by the facts of human life, the words here quoted show the danger those are in who surrender themselves blindly to those forces, which from Machiavelli through Hobbes and Bodin have come to be dominant in politics, and are at this moment dangerously ascendant owing to the horror of that very economic and industrial oppression which is the distinctive gift of modern capitalism to history. In this country, however, few are likely to go quite so far as M. Combes. Owing partly to the continuance of ideas that have come down from the Middle Ages, partly to the struggles of the seventeenth century, the

notion of individual liberty is very strong.
Individual rights of conscience are recognised—even in such matters as public health.
And though there are not wanting indica-
tions that this sentiment is very much on
the wane, it is still the case, that so far
as principle goes, few English statesmen
could deny the authority of the individual
conscience.   At the same time, utterances
like those of M. Combes and certain move-
ments violent at this moment in England
should prevent our being too certain in this
matter.   Entire capitulation to this prevailing tendency to deify the State, if only in
the matter of corporate institutions, will
in the long run be no more favourable to
individual liberty than the so-called "free-
labour" movement organised by capitalists
is likely to be to the economic freedom
of the artisan classes.   Yet our concern, as
I showed last time, is not with individual,
but rather with corporate liberty.

And here I have no doubt that objections
will be raised.   How, it will be asked, can
you say that we need to do battle for
the rights of corporations when already the
country is groaning under their tyranny,

and the law of limited companies is the cover under which is carried every form of that exploitation which, if conducted by millionaires, is known as "high finance," and if practised by their clerks is called by a different name? I am not denying that corporate societies exist, or that they exist in large numbers; no complex state of civilisation can exist without this phenomenon appearing; and if it appears, the law must somehow or other take account of it. What is wrong is not the fact but the nature of existence allowed to these bodies in legal theory. Any corporate body, in the ordinary and not the technical sense, of a society of men bound together for a permanent interest inevitably acts with that unity and sense of direction which we attribute to personality. The question is, how is this personality to be conceived? Is it a natural fact, the expression of the social union; or is it merely something artificial imposed upon the body for its own convenience by the State? Is it real or fictitious, this legal personality? Under the dominant theory the corporate person is a fiction, a *nomen juris;* in order that societies of men may be able to act, to hold property, to sue and be sued, it is necessary to treat them as what they are not, *i.e.* as persons; therefore the sovereign power by its own act grants to such bodies as it pleases the name of corporation, and with it endows them with a "fictitious" personality; since, however, it is a mere matter of convenient imagination on the part of the law, and corresponds to no reality in the collective body, its entire genesis and right are merely a delegation of the sovereign authority. All corporations owe their existence to a grant or concession of the State, tacit if not express, which may be given or withheld. Other societies, if they exist at all, are purely contractual, and have no such power of suing or being sued. They are *collegia* or *societates*, not "universities." The Romans approached, though they did not entirely reach, this position.[1] The final word was really said by

---

[1] So wurde schliesslich die römische Jurisprudenz unabweislich zu der Annahme gedrängt, dass die Persönlichkeit der *Universitas*—eine Fiktion sei. Zwar haben die Römer diesen Gedanken weder mit Einem Schlage noch überhaupt im voller Schärfe formulirt, geschweige denn über Natur und Inhalt dieses Fik-

the great canonist Sinibaldo Fieschi, afterwards Pope Innocent IV. With the large
number of cathedral chapters and religious
orders in the Church, it became very necessary to arrive at clear views on the matter,
and Innocent IV, starting from the doctrine
of the civil law as to the nature of sovereign
power and the rights of individuals, came
quite definitely to the view that it was
necessary to call such bodies persons; but
that their personality was purely fictitious,
nomen juris, and therefore entirely within

tion theoretische Erwägungen angestellt. Allein der
gesammte Aufbau ihres Korporationsrechts gipfelte
in dem Satz, dass hier von positiven Recht eine
Nichtperson personificirt sei. (Gierke, *op. cit.*, iii.
103.)

Cf. also the following :—

Als publicistisches Wesen war die *Universitas*—
eine reale Einheit aber keine Person. Als Privat-
rechtssubject war sie eine Person, aber keine reale
Einheit. Eine wirkliche Person war nur der Mensch,
weil nur er ein Individuum und nur das Individuum
Person war. Wenn eine *Universitas* obwohl sie ihren
realen Substrat nach kein Individuum war, als Person
und somit als Individuum gesetzt wurde, so lag
darin die vom Recht vollzogene Behandlung einer in
Wirklichkeit nicht existenten Thatsache, als sei sie
existent. (Gierke, iii. 103.)

Der Verbandsbegriff der römischen Jurisprudenz.

the power of the prince.[1] Under the influences which led to the reception of the
Roman Civil Law in Germany and its
dominance throughout Western Europe,
this view developed into the full doctrine
of the concession theory of corporate life.
Although Roman Law, as such, was never
accepted in England, yet through the influence of chancellors trained partly as
canonists, and through the general develop-

[1] Derselbe Papst (Innocent III) verbot zugleich
wegen der gesteigerten Mannichfaltigkeit der Kongre-
gationen die Begründung neuer Orden, ein Verbot,
von dem freilich bald darauf zu Gunsten der Bettel-
mönche wieder abgegangen wurden musste, das aber
doch deutlich zeigt *wie auch dem gewaltigen Aufsschwung
der religiösen Association* gegenüber die Kirche an dem
Standpunkt festhielt, dass die Existenz einer geistlichen Genossenschaft von der päpstlichen Sanktion
abhängig sei. In der That setzte jetzt wie später die
Kirche es durch, das alle neu entstehenden geistlichen
Gesellschaften von einiger Bedeutung ihrer Regel und
Verfassung sich—formell wenigstens—vom päpstlichen
Stuhle ertheilen liessen und von ihm die Gesammtheit
ihrer Rechte herleiteten, so dass auch die spons-
tansten Ordensvereinigungen ebenso wie die einzelnen
Ordensgemeinden nie unter den Begriff völlig freier
Gesellschaften fielen, sondern als kirchliche Anstalten
mit gesellschaftlicher Verfassung betrachtet wurden.
(Gierke, i. 293.)

ment of absolutism in the sixteenth century, a view substantially the same became prevalent in this country, and is still the official doctrine, although more and more influences are tending in the opposite direction. The present state of affairs can be seen from the perusal of the inaugural lecture at Oxford of Dr. Geldart on *Legal Personality*. An instance of the way in which facts are proving too strong for it, was the judgment in the *Taff Vale Case* confirmed by the House of Lords. In order to save their funds from certain dangers, the Acts which enfranchised the *Trades Unions in* 1875, and relieved them from the law of conspiracy, had expressly denied to them the character of corporations. Thus the common chest of the union could not be raided for any illegal acts of its agents. In the *Taff Vale Case*, however, it was decided, that though they were not corporate bodies legally, yet since their acts were of a nature so closely akin to those of persons, so far as the question of damages was concerned they were to be treated as such, and made responsible for the acts of agents. Outcries were raised against this judgment, which was certainly contrary to what had for nearly a generation been supposed to be the law ; and eventually the *Trades Disputes Act* was passed to relieve the unions in regard to picketing. This, however, is irrelevant. Whatever other influences may have assisted in forming the minds of the judges, the truth is that the judgment bears witness to the fact that corporate personality, this unity of life and action, is a thing which grows up naturally and inevitably in bodies of men united for a permanent end, and that it cannot in the long run be denied merely by the process of saying that it is not there. In other words, this personality is inherent in the nature of the society as such, and is not a mere name to be granted or denied at the pleasure of the sovereign authority. That so much was actually declared by the House of Lords, I do not say ; but that this was the inner meaning of their decision seems undoubted. On the other hand, in the Osborne judgment the old prejudice must have been largely at the bottom of the decision, which forbad to the unions the power to use their funds as a whole to pay Members of Parliament. In other words, the members of the union are a mere collection of individuals, who are unchanged by their membership of the society, and cannot therefore have the funds subscribed turned to a purpose to which, though even in a minority, they object. A similar view is at the bottom of a recent decision about the power of a club to raise its subscription. A well-known London club attempted to do this; one of the members refused to pay the additional amount, and was expelled in consequence. He brought an action, and the courts decided in his favour, *i.e.* that it was all a matter of contract, and that the club had no authority, no real inherent life, which could enable it to pass beyond the arrangements made with the individual member at his election, who might thus enjoy every kind of new improvement or addition to the club without paying his share in the extra cost.

So long as this doctrine or anything like it be dominant, it would probably be an evil rather than a benefit if the Church of England were to become, what it now is not, a corporation recognised as such by the law. For that would under existing condi-

E

tions mean that it was subject to all sorts of restrictions, while at the same time it would still be denied inherent rights of self-development. True, facts are always stronger than abstract theories, and the fact of corporate life might not improbably be too strong for any legal theories which denied it. This was the case in the Scotch instance. But at present this could hardly be guaranteed. On the other hand, it was shown in a very interesting essay of Maitland,[1] that part of the practical difficulty has been solved in this country by the institution of trusts. Under cover of trusteeship, a great deal of action has taken place which is really that of corporate personality, without the society being subject to the disabilities incident to the "concession theory." He points out in regard to the Inns of Court, which, being bodies of lawyers, may be supposed to know what is their interest, that they have always refused incorporation, finding that they can under the doctrine of trusteeship do what they want and have most of the safeguards without the disabilities of corporate life.

---

[1] *Collected Papers,* vol. iii. pp. 321–404.

At the same time, it was probably through the lack of a proper corporate recognition that a scandal was possible, like that by which the property of Serjeant's Inn could be treated as the individual possession of its existing members and divided up between them. The essay is very interesting and valuable, for it shows how the practical good sense of Englishmen has enabled them to accept an abstract doctrine of the nature of the corporation, not germane to the realities of life, while denuding it of many of its most grievous consequences.

It may seem that these considerations are matters merely of legal theory, and that they do not concern us in the practical problem of securing reasonable liberty for the Church as a self-developing body. I think that this is not the case. For let us consider what is at the back of it all. Since the corporate society is only a *persona ficta*, with the name given it by the law, but no real inward life, we have on this view but two social entities, the State on the one hand and the individual on the other. The rights or actions of the one are private, those of the other are public. The State may be of any kind of structure, monarchic, aristocratic, or purely collectivist; but in all cases there are recognised by the law, no real social entities, no true powers, except the sovereign on the one hand with irresistible authority, and the mass of individuals on the other. Societies, so far as they exist, are mere collections of individuals who remain unchanged by their membership, and whose unity of action is narrowly circumscribed by the State, and where allowed is allowed on grounds quite arbitrary. Under such a view there can be no possible place for the religious body, in the sense of a Church living a supernatural life, and the claim is quite just that no Church should have any standard of morals different from those of the State.

But is not this woefully to misconceive the actual facts of social life, as they present themselves to our eyes, and to get a wrong notion of the State? Let me give an instance. Throughout the education controversy much has been heard against the iniquity of privately managed schools receiving public money, at least in the form of rates (for the income-tax is not concerned with conscience). Now surely (except in the case of the one-man manager) this is a total misconception. As opposed to State management, perhaps the word private may be admitted, but when it implies, as it ought, purely individual management, a false view is suggested. These social bodies other than the State are not only not private, but in their working they are more akin to the State than they are to the individual. I mean that both of them are cases of a society acting as one, to which the individual members are subject. The relations between the member and his society are more akin to those of a citizen to a State than to anything in the individual. It is very easy to say that universities, colleges, trade unions, inns of court, &c. &c., are purely private, and in one sense it is true; they are not delegates of the State or parts of its machinery; but they are in a very real sense public, *i.e.* they are collective, not individual, in their constitution. The popular use of the word " Public School " to denote a school under collective management is a far more reasonable and realistic habit, though I suppose that it is not technically justified. The point is that it is the public communal character of all such institutions that is the salient fact; and that we do wrong to adopt a rigid division into public and private, if we mean by the latter any and every institution that is not a delegation from the State. What we actually see in the world is not on the one hand the State, and on the other a mass of unrelated individuals; but a vast complex of gathered unions, in which alone we find individuals, families, clubs, trades unions, colleges, professions, and so forth; and further, that there are exercised functions within these groups which are of the nature of government, including its three aspects, legislative, executive, and judicial; though, of course, only with reference to their own members. So far as the people who actually belong to it are concerned, such a body is every whit as communal in its character as a municipal corporation or a provincial parliament.

Not only, however, is this view false to the true character of the State; it is entirely wrong in its view of the individual citizen. As a matter of fact, personality is a social fact; no individual could ever come to himself except as a member of a society, and the membership of any society does not leave even the adult individual where he was. There is an interpenetration of his life with that of the society, and his personality is constantly being changed by this fellowship. Too often on the part of those who strongly believe in human personality, the necessities of controversy against doctrines which virtually deny it has led to an insistence on the individual to the neglect of the social side. Correction of this error will be found in a very valuable book by Mr. Wilfrid Richmond, *Personality as a Philosophical Principle.* We cannot, however, too often emphasize in regard to politics, that not the individual but the family is the real social unit, and that personality as a fact never grows up except within one or more social unions. That, however, will be met by the claim that this is just what citizenship means ; that " the State is prior " to the individual, and that true personality is to grow up in the great collective union of national life. This seems to me to lie at the root of the difficulty.

When Aristotle uttered his famous dictum,

the State meant, as all know, a small body of persons, not more than could be gathered in one place; and although we may hold that the antique State was too all-embracing, at least it was not unreasonable to maintain that the compact City-State of ancient Greece was the social home of all the individuals comprising it, and no more was needed. In the modern world, however, no such assertion is possible. Whatever the State may attempt, she cannot be the mother of all her citizens in the same sense as the City-State of old ; and, as a fact, men will grow to maturity and be moulded in their prejudices, their tastes, their capacities, and their moral ideals not merely by the great main stream of national life, but also, and perhaps more deeply, by their own family connections, their local communal life in village or town, their educational society (for it is of the essence of education to be in a society), and countless other collective organisms. It is these that make up the life of the modern world, and to deny them all real existence or power, whether it be in the interests of legal theory or of an abstract economic collectivism, seems to me to be in principle false to the facts, and in practice to be steering straight for the rocks. It must not be forgotten that on the ideal system which arose out of the Greek City-State the fact of the family as a real entity disappears ; and Plato would allow a community in wives.

What has really happened is that a conception of sovereignty which more or less expressed the facts in the ancient City-State was extended to the vast world-empire of the Romans, developed and concentrated in the autocrat at its head. The doctrine of the unity of the sovereign power and the complete non-existence of all other real authorities became the settled presupposition of the lawyers, and crystallised into maxims which are familiar to all, such as *quod principi placuit legis habet vigorem*, that the Emperor was *legibus solutus*, and so forth. Moreover, the fact that there remained in the account of the *lex regia* a tradition of the popular origin of the Imperial authority has rendered it more easy to apply the same doctrine to a modern State. Whether or no, as the *lex regia* implies, all power was originally in the

people, who' transferred it by irrevocable
act to the prince, it is equally clear that
the essential doctrine of a single irresistible
authority "inalienable, indivisible, and incapable of legal limitation " is ready to hand
in the Roman system, and may be applied
with equal facility to a modern democracy
like France or an ancient empire like Rome.
In either case it is equally destructive of
any real recognition of the rights of social
unions other than the State.   Except as its
own delegations, the Imperial Government
was extremely suspicious of all such societies;
and, as I have said, it treated corporations
in a way which differed from the more developed " concession theory " only in that it
had not reached so far even as the notion
that they were fictitious persons.   But the
point is that of all real life in such bodies
the Government was most suspicious, and
Sir William Ramsay in his *Church and the
Roman Empire* has shown that it was just
in this fact, that the Church claimed a different sanction, a separate life, and a new
non-Roman unity, that lay the whole ground
of the long persecution.   Unfortunately,
when the Church triumphed, she for the

time virtually abandoned the claim to freedom within the State which had deluged
the Coliseum with blood. There was no
change in the antique Græco-Roman
conception of a single all-absorbing omnicompetent power, the source of every right,
and facing with no intermediates the vast
masses of individual citizens. The only
difference made was that this State from
being Pagan became Christian, and after
the proscription of Paganism by Theodosius the Great there was no need for
men to worry themselves with forming a
totally new doctrine of the structure of
civil society. The *De Civitate Dei* of St.
Augustine provided the framework in which
all the political thinking of men was done
for more than a thousand years, nor is its
influence even yet extinct. The mediæval
doctrine of the *Holy Roman Empire* crystallised this ideal in a form which, if not
very practicable, was at least an object to
work for, and did as a fact direct the life
and work of many of its greatest leaders.
An ideal which Charles the Great, Otho the
Great, Pope Sylvester II, Henry of Luxem-
burg were content even to try to realise

cannot be dismissed as of no influence on the lives of men. If it was not realised, it at least caused people to do what they would otherwise have left undone and ruled their imaginations, a fact which is plain from Dante's *De Monarchia* and from many of the most striking passages in the *Divina Commedia.*

On the other hand, the Teutonic polity and habit of mind, if it did not quite produce, approached a view of the relation of the individual to the society and of the smaller societies to the whole, which is that to which we are being driven. The enormous development of corporate life in the Middle Ages, guilds of every kind, and the whole notion of the system of estates in the body politic all testified to the same fact. There was a very definite sense of the individual, not as something separate, but as moulded and interpenetrated by the life of the society. There was, further, the very definite sense that the societies all were organic, that they lived by an inherent spontaneity of life, and that as communal societies they had their own rights and liberty, which did not originate in the grant of the sovereign. As Gierke, however, points out, this was instinctive rather than theoretical; they had not reached the difficult and developed conception of corporate personality. And this, among many other causes, is the explanation of the ease with which the ancient ideas of corporate liberty and real social life went down before the logically developed and erudite system which ruled the minds of the lawyers from the Renaissance onwards.[1]

Nor must it be supposed that the Church was an exception. The theory of the Church came from the Roman Empire. Neither Churchmen nor statesmen believed in two separate social entities, the Church and the State, each composed of the same persons. Nor indeed was that necessary in the mediæval idea of a Christian State. Rather, when conflict is spoken of between Church and State, it is conflict between two bodies of officials, the civil and the

---

[1] An interesting account of the contrast between the learned, gentlemanly Roman system and the ancient Teutonic communal law will be found in the essay of the Germanist, Georg Beseler, *Volksrecht und Juristenrecht.*

ecclesiastical. When Henry IV resisted Hildebrand, he admitted that for the case of heresy he might be deposed; and the whole atmosphere of the mediæval mind was such that we cannot picture them as treating the two as really separate societies. When the liberty of the Church is claimed, it almost always denotes the liberty of the hierarchy, not that of the whole body. Alike on the Imperial and the Papal side, the claims raised would have been inconceivable, had it not been admitted that both Popes and Emperors were rulers in one society. I do not say that there was no approximation to the idea of a "free Church in a free State"; but so long as persecution was taken for granted, and a coercive Church-State was the ideal, the claims which we put forward were not seriously entertained. That was the root of the difficulty.

With the then existing presuppositions and the argument from abstract unity so strong—strong partly because of the universal lawlessness—the claim to freedom, whether put forward by the civil or the ecclesiastical power, became inevitably a claim to supremacy, and was therefore never really admitted by the others. The Popes could never allow that matters of religion and conscience were to be at the mercy of politicians; the Emperors could never allow that the State merely existed on sufferance of the spiritual power. This conflict could never be solved so long as both parties maintained the right and duty of persecution, *i.e.* the necessary connection of membership of the Church with citizenship in the State. Furthermore, inside the polity of the Church, the other system had triumphed and the development of the Papal system meant the transference to the Pope of all the notions of illimitable authority claimed by the Emperor in truth. The great *Leviathan* of Hobbes, the *plenitudo potestatis* of the canonists, the *arcana imperii*, the sovereignty of Austin, are all names of the same thing—the unlimited and illimitable power of the law-giver in the State, deduced from the notion of its unity. It makes no difference whether it is the State or the Church that is being considered.

Towards the close of the Middle Ages it

might seem as though the way was being paved for a more natural system. So far as the European monarchs were concerned, the Imperial claim remained no more than honorific, and after the conflict between Philippe le Bel and Boniface VIII there seemed no possibility of asserting claims of the Papacy against the rising national powers.. Within those national powers, institutions had arisen all over Europe, which expressed the fact that the State was a *communitas communitatum*. This is the true meaning of our word Commons; not the mass of the common people, but the community of the communities. However imperfect in theory, there was a practical recognition of merchant and craft guilds, with borough charters, guild liberties, the baronial honours, with courts Christian, courts royal, and courts manor, all function-ing, with special laws and customs recognised even for fairs and markets and universities. These facts, together with the traditions of fellowship life coming down from a long past, might well make it seem that a system of universal liberties and balanced powers would result, that at last the lion

of the throne would lie down with the lamb
of spiritual freedom in a semi-federalist
polity.

But it was not to be. The lion got outside of the lamb. Roman Law became
more and more the norm; 1495 is the date
of its reception in Germany; national and
local customs were decried by the civilians,
learned, classical, Romanist to the core.
The dangers of anarchy under feudalism
made the mass of men blind to the dangers
of autocracy. All the learning of the Renaissance was in favour of the power of
the prince, save for a few dreamers who
looked to a republic. Clerical immunities
had been abused; the religious orders were
too much of an *imperium in imperio*. With
the Lutheran movement, there went on the
one hand the destruction of the ancient
conception of Christendom as a single polity,
under the leadership of Pope and Emperor
and the Lordship of Christ; and on the
other, the transference to the prince as
head of a compact territorial unity of the
bulk of the prerogatives of both spiritual
and secular power. The doctrine of *cujus
regio ejus religio* of the religious peace of

Augsburg was the natural expression of this fact; so that one elector could say quite readily that his people's conscience belonged to him. That was, of course, the notion of Henry VIII. It was formulated into a complete theory of the State by Jean Bodin in France, and afterwards by Thomas Hobbes in England. Hobbes denied every kind of right not derived from the sovereign; and devotes one book of his *Leviathan* to "the kingdom of darkness," in other words the Roman Church, which he thus denominates because its claims would break up the unity of the sovereign power. In the seventeenth century, both in England and on the Continent, this notion of a compact omnicompetent sovereign, by whose permission alone existed the right to breathe, was mixed up with the theory of the divine right of kings. But it is not really tied thereto. The eighteenth century saw it asserted of Parliament; and the claim to parliamentary omnipotence was the real cause of the American Revolution. In the other hemisphere was set up a State which, as being federal, was largely a denial of this claim;

but the civil war seems to have proved the contrary. Even now, however, the doctrine of State rights is still strong, is said to be gaining rather than losing adherents, and we may learn much from the attitude of the American courts to such problems as those of the free development of religious bodies.

In France, unlike England, the theory of sovereignty had been crystallised in the person of the monarch; but it was not overthrown by the Revolution. What was overthrown was the surviving remnant of feudalism and the last relics of local and partial liberty. The doctrine of a single uniform all-absorbing power has been carried to a height further than even Louis XIV could have dreamed; and, as we have seen, even religious toleration exists only in name. This doctrine has found in England classical expression in the writings of John Austin, which do little more than formulate the Roman theory of sovereignty, and is imbued with the same notion of the entire distinction between public and private, which forbids any right classification of social institutions. Austin has been subjected to much criticism, but with certain slight qualifications his notions still rule the legal mind—except, of course, those who are definitely working towards a new doctrine of corporate life. And in regard to the Church, and to morals alike, it is taken as an axiom that the law is morally binding, and by many that what is legally right cannot be morally wrong.

This doctrine is, however, becoming more and more difficult to reconcile with the facts. As a mere verbal theory I do not know that this view of sovereign power is assailable ; and by means of the proviso that whatever the sovereign permits he commands, we cannot positively say that any measure of freedom is inconsistent with it. Practically, however, it is clear that we need something different and more profound. We have seen one salient instance of the pitfalls it is apt to lead to. We must bear in mind that Parliament is nominally sovereign, not only in England but in every portion of the Empire, and that no local liberty exists in theory but as a delegated authority for the will of the Imperial Parliament. Yet in regard to the immigration law in South Africa, it was admitted that the Imperial Parliament dare not override the will of the local bodies even though they were doing a manifest injustice to their fellow-subjects. In other words, the local body had a real independent life, and could not be touched.

The theory of government which is at the root of all the trouble is briefly this. All and every right is the creation of the one and indivisible sovereign; whether the sovereign be a monarch or an assembly is not material. No prescription, no conscience, no corporate life can be pleaded against its authority, which is without legal limitation. In every State there must be some power entirely above the law, because it can alter the law. To talk of rights as against it is to talk nonsense. In so far as every State is a State, this view is held to be not only true but self-evident. In so far as it is not true, it is because the State is in a condition of incipient dissolution and anarchy is already setting in. The doctrine of sovereignty is, in fact, a deduction partly from the universality of law in a stable commonwealth, and partly from the abstract

notion of unity.   That this latter has much
to do with it will be evident to all who are
acquainted with the controversialist literature of either the Middle Ages or the
seventeenth century.   Filmer's *Anarchy of
a Mixed Monarchy* is a brief statement of
this standpoint.

But the truth is, that this State in a
sense of absolute superhuman unity has
never really existed, and that it cannot
exist.   In theory it represents a despot
ruling over slaves; in practice even a despot
is limited by the fact that slaves are, after
all, human; deny their personality as you
like, there comes a point at which it asserts
itself, and they will kill either the despot
or themselves.   At bottom the doctrine
represents a State, which is a super-man
ruling individuals who are below men.   It
is like the absolute of the Bradleyan philosophy which absorbs and ultimately anni-
hilates all individual distinction.   It is
partly symbolised by the title-page of the
Leviathan of Hobbes.   Attempts are made
to get out of the difficulty by saying that
the sovereign power, though theoretically
illimitable, is limited in practice very mate-

rially ; psychologically by its own nature, and externally by the fact that there are certain things which no government can do without provoking resistance, *e.g.* Louis XIV could not have established Mohammedanism, even if he had wished. In this way custom on the one hand, local liberties or individual rights on the other, would acquire a place. We are, I admit, brought nearer to the facts.[1] But it seems a weakness in a doctrine that you can only fit the facts into its framework by making such serious qualifications, and it would appear a more reasonable maxim to get a theory of law and government not by laying down an abstract doctrine of unity, but by observing the facts of life as it is lived, and trying to set down the actual features of civil society. What do we find as a fact ? Not, surely, a sand-heap of individuals, all equal and undifferentiated, unrelated except to the State, but an ascending hierarchy of groups, family, school, town, county, union, Church, &c. &c. All these groups (or many of them) live with

[1] This view is most lucidly stated by Professor Dicey in *The Law of the Constitution*, pp. 72–81.

a real life; they act towards one another with a unity of will and mind as though they were single persons; they all need to be allowed reasonable freedom, but must be restrained from acts of injustice towards one another or the individual; they are all means by which the individual comes to himself. For in truth the notion of isolated individuality is the shadow of a dream, and would never have come into being but for the vast social structure which allows a few individuals to make play, as though they were independent, when their whole economic position of freedom is symbolic of a long history and complex social organisation. In the real world, the isolated individual does not exist; he begins always as a member of something, and, as I said earlier, his personality can develop only in society, and in some way or other he always embodies some social institution. I do not mean to deny the distinctness of individual life, but this distinction can function only inside a society. Membership in a social union means a direction of personality, which interpenetrates it, and, according to your predilection, you may call either an extension or a narrowing; it is in truth both. You cannot be a member of any society and be the same as though you were not a member; it affects your rights and duties, limits at once and increases your opportunities, and makes you a different being, although in many different degrees, according to the nature of the society and the individual member. You are not merely John Doe or Richard Roe, but as John may probably be a member of the Christian Church by baptism, a Doe by family, an Englishman by race; all three are social institutions, which have grown into you. In addition to this you are a member of a school, an alumnus of a college, a sharer in this club, a president of that, and so forth. All these groups and unions have their effect, and limit and develop your life, make you do, or refrain from doing, what otherwise you would not, and in so far prevent you being a free and un-trammelled citizen of the State. More than that, they penetrate your imagination and your thought and alter not only what you do but what you want to do. Between all these groups there will be relations, and not merely between the individuals composing them. To prevent injustice between them and to secure their rights, a strong power above them is needed. It is largely to regulate such groups and to ensure that they do not outstep the bounds of justice that the coercive force of the State exists. It does not create them; nor is it in many matters in direct and immediate contact with the individual. The claim of the Church in matters of education is the claim that she shall be recognised as a group, in which the natural authority over its members extends to the provision of a social atmosphere; and this ought to be admitted, provided the requirements of citizenship in secular culture be provided and controlled.

All this, it will be said, lessens the hold of the State over the individual. But this is needful the moment you reach any large and complex society. In a developed state of civilisation many interests must be allowed social expression, which in one sense are a separating influence. Even a member of a musical club is so far separated from those who are excluded; and he is changed by the fact of this club-life, which enters into him. In the Middle Ages there was an appropriate dress for every calling; under the modern notion we have all been trying to dress alike, and most of us doing it very badly. The old custom survives in clergy and in butcher boys, and we are seeing revivals in the costumes of boy scouts. Instead of an iron uniformity, we need more and more a reasonable distinction of groups, all of which should be honourable. There is a whole philosophy in school colours.

Recent discussions are making men ask once more in matters other than religion, what are the limits of the authority of Parliament? The idolatry of the State is receiving shrewd blows. It is said, however, especially in regard to the Church, that to recognise its rights is dangerous. But if it is a fact, it must be more dangerous not to recognise its real life. The same is true of individuals. However you may proclaim with M. Combes that "there are no rights but the rights of the State," you find individuals who habitually act as if they had them; and even when you go on to say that "there is no authority but the authority of the republic," you do not in practice prevent all kinds of societies from behaving in a way that implies authority over their members. Nor can you. It is impossible. Society is inherent in human nature, and that means inevitably the growth of a communal life and social ties; nor is it possible to confine this to the single society we call the State, unless it be on a very small scale, and even then there is the family to reckon with. Of course such societies may come into collision with the State; so may individuals. Always there is a possibility of civil war. But you will not escape the possibility by ignoring the facts. The only way to be sure an individual will never become a criminal is to execute him; the only way to secure a State from all danger on the part of its members is to have none. Every State is a synthesis of living wills. Harmony must ever be a matter of balance and adjustment, and this at any moment might be upset, owing to the fact that man is a spiritual being and not a mere automaton. It would seem to be wiser to treat all these great and small corporate entities which make up our national life as real, as living beings, *i.e.* practically as persons, and then when this is once realised, limit them in their action, than it is to try and treat them as what they are not, *i.e.* as dead bodies, dry bones, into which nothing but an arbitrary fiat gives a simulacrum of life, which may at any moment be withdrawn. After all, the Roman Government did not destroy the living unity of the Church by denying its claim to exist; but it nearly destroyed itself in the attempt.

Note

The following excerpts from Gierke are valuable in this connection. The first shows how, in Gierke's view, the great difference between the Teutonic and the Latin mind lay in the fact that the one starts from the idea of Law, the other from that of Force. The second shows how the ancient view by a too literal use of the personification of the State was driven to that artificial conception of unity we were discussing. Another shows how Roman Law superadded to

Greek the notion of the free individual, always in Roman idea a tyrant ruling over slaves. It would be interesting to inquire how much of the evils of the extremer individualism are due to the survivals of a State theory generated by the fact that the "full-free" citizen was legally a tyrant in his "familia." The next passage traces a part of the growth of the full conception of the State, as it developed in the communal life of mediæval Europe. It is this which, according to Gierke, rather than the kingdom or the empire, affords the most valuable lessons to the political student. Finally, another citation gives Gierke's own views of the true conception of the State:

Während die Griechische wie die römische Geschichte mit dem Staate beginnt, beginnt die Germanische mit dem Recht.

Jedenfalls ist es gewiss, dass bei uns in die wirkliche Welt wie in das Bewusstsein *der Staat sehr viel später als das Recht trat.*

Es gab im Grunde weder öffentliches noch privates, sondern nur ein einziges, einartiges Recht. Aber dieses Recht war durch und durch Recht; es trug in allen seinen Theilen die Merkmale der Gegenseitigkeit, und Erzwingbarkeit an sich; es war vollkommen selbständig und sogar so selbständig, dass es seinerseits

alles staatliche Leben band. Öffentliche wie private
Verhältnisse wurden so mit dem Stempel der Einen
Rechtsidee ausgeprägt. (Gierke, ii. 32.)

Der Staat ist dem Menschen gleichartig und er
unterscheidet sich von ihm nur wie das Grössere vom
Kleineren, er ist um so vollkommener, je mehr er
sich durch seine Organisation dem Menschen nähert.
Hieraus, ergibt sich die Anforderung einer Einheit des
Staats, welche gleich der des Individuums möglichst
einfach ist; einer Einheit in welcher die Theile ganz
enthalten und nur für das Ganze werthvoll sind,
einer Einheit, die zuletzt zum Kommunismus drängt.
(Gierke, iii. 15.)

Gehörte zur welthistorischen Mission der Römer die
Schöpfung des ersten Privatrechts so war in demselben Sinne in der welthistorischen Mission der Germanen die erste Schöpfung des öffentlichen Rechts
enthalten. Bei den Griechen war alles Recht im
Verhältniss zum Staat unfrei, es gieng nicht blos der
Bürger im Staat, sondern das Individuum im Burger
auf; die Römer setzen das Privatrecht selbständig
gegen den Staat und gaben demselben Menschen, der
als Bürger im Staat, aufgieng eine individuelle Sphäre
souveräner Willensmacht; die Germanen zuerst er-
klärten auch die Beziehungen zwischen Staat und
Bürgern für Recht, und schufen das öffentliche Recht
als Bestandtheil des Einen Rechtes, das überall sich
selber gleich blieb. (Gierke, ii. 32.)

Die Stadtpersonlichkeit. Das öffentliche Recht
wurde nicht durch den absoluten Willen eines dem
Bürger gegenüber schrankenlosen Staatsgewalt als von
aussen kommende unabänderliche Zwangsnorm hinge-
stellt; es war vielmehr das gesetz welches der dem
bürgerlichen Organismus immanente und von allen

seinen Gliedern getragene Gemeinwille sich selber setzte. Daher wurde denn auch die Stetigkeit des öffentlichen Rechts vor Erstarrung dadurch gewahrt, dass der freien Selbstbestimmung und dem bewussten Entschluss des öffentlichen Willens die Änderung anheimgestellt und überdies auch innerhalb des objectiv fest gestellten Rahmens ein bestimmtes Bewegungsfeld frei gelassen ward. Im Gegensatz zu dem von der Vielheit der Individuen ausgehenden Privatrecht gieng allerdings das öffentliche Recht von der Einheit des Gemeinwesens aus; *aber dieses Gemein wesen war ein Organismus, dessen Gliederung und Organisation selbst unter das Recht fiel.* Deshalb erzeugte auch für den von ihm geregelten Kreis das öffentliche Recht *keineswegs nur einseitige Befugnisse der Stadt als solcher und willenlose Unterwerfung der Bürger;* sondern es erzeugte gegenseitige Beziehungen zwischen dem Ganzen und seinen Theilen, *die als Glieder einer höheren Einheit dennoch zugleich selbständige Einheiten blieben.* So war es möglich trotz der Erhebung der Stadt zum Staat die Rechtsnatur des öffentlichen Rechtes beizubehalten und demselben trotz der Emancipation vom Privatrechtsbegriff vollen gerichtlichen Schutz zu gewähren. (Gierke, ii. 646.)

Der Staatsbegriff.

Der Staat ist die Person gewordene höchst Allgemeinheit. Er unterscheidet sich daher von allen anderen Verbandsperson dadurch dass es nichts ihm Aehnliches mehr über ihm gibt. Er ist aber andrerseits nur das letzte Glied in der Reihe der zu Personen entwickelten Verbände, indem er gleich ihnen den verbunden Individuen gegenüber den gemeinheitlichen Willen zur rechtlichen Einheit verkörpert.

Der Staatsbegriff ist daher zwar nicht der *Gegensatz*

*des Körperschaftsbegriffes, aber er ist weiter und enger
als dieser.* Er ist weiter weil er nicht nur als höchste
Steigerung des körperschaftsbegriffes, sondern auch
als höchste Steigerung des Anstaltsbegriffes zur Erscheinung kommen oder auch Korporative und anstaltliche Momente in sich verschmelzen kann. Er ist aber
anderseits enger, weil der Körperschaftsbegriff eine
Reihe weiterer Merkmale in sich aufnehmen müssen, um
zum Staatsbegriff zu werden. *Der Staat kann also Körperschaft sein, kann aber auch jedes Korporativen Charakters
entbehren. Die Körperschaft aber wird nothwendig zum
Staat,* sobald sie als höchster und umfassendster Ver-
band auf einen bestimmten Gebiet für Erreichung des
menschlichen Gemeinschaftswerkes schlechtin kon-
stituirt ist. Der korporative Staat lässt sich als
staatliches Gemeinwesen, der anstaltliche Staat als
Obrigkeitsstaat bezeichnen, dazwischen aber lässt sich
in mannichfacher Weise eine Kombination korpora-
tives und anstaltlicher Elemente als Erscheinungsform
der Staatsidee vorstellen.

Weil es zu alten Zeiten Verbände über den Einzelnen
gab, immer aber unter diesen Verbänden ein höchster
sein musste, existirte Staatliches von je. Allein der
Staat blieb, so lange die Verbandspersönlichkeit
sich mit der Rechtssubjectivät eines Herrn oder
eine Gesammtheit deckte, in seinen sinnlichen
Trägern latent. Der Staat als Person war weder in
das Bewusstsein noch in das Leben getreten, und es
fehlte folgeweise an einer selbständigen und nur
durch ihr eignes inneres Wesen bestimmten Staats-
existenz. Das Staatliche kam nirgend für sich und
rein, sondern überall in konkreter Bindung und zu-
fälliger Trübung durch Individuelles zur Erscheinung.
Sobald indess irgendwo die einen bestimmten Ver-

band durchdringende Einheit als Person gesetzt war, musste insoweit, als diese Einheit die in ihrer Art höchste war, der Staatsbegriff gegeben sein. Insbesondere musste sich daher auch der Körperschaftsbegriff, wenn einmal entwickelt, auf seiner jeweilig höchsten Stufe sofort zum Staatsbegriff steigern.

So war denn in der That die Stadt, weil sie die erste und zunächst in ihrer Art höchste Körperschaft war, zugleich der älteste wahre und für sich bestehende deutsche Staat. Der Staatsbegriff aber kam an ihr in der besonderen form des bürgerlichen Gemeinwesen zur Erscheinung. (Gierke, ii. 831.)

LECTURE III

THE CIVIC STANDPOINT

So far our course has been clear. We have seen that the essential minimum of any claim we make for the Church must depend on its recognition as a social union with an inherent original power of self-development, acting as a person with a mind and will of its own. All other matters between Church and State are questions of detail; and there is room for mutual concession. What is not a detail but a principle is that which I have put forward, and we have seen that this is not granted; that it is opposed by the prevailing opinion of State omnipotence entrenched in popular thought, and still more so in the opinion of lawyers; that the doctrine to which we are opposed is no novelty, nor is it specifically modern, but that it owes its force to the continuance of age-long traditions, to the survival of the

State idea of the ancient world related most completely to the Athens of Aristotle, but developed and heightened with all the majesty of Imperial Rome, and inherent in the Canon no less than the Civil Law. Further, we have seen that this false conception of the State as the only true political entity apart from the individual is at variance not only with ecclesiastical liberty, but with the freedom of all other communal life, and ultimately with that of the individual ; moreover, that it is fast breaking down under the pressure of the historical jurists like Dr. Gierke and Maitland, and the fact of the innumerable developments of the associative instinct and of the positive political facts of a modern world-empire. All these developments are facts ; although it may not be impossible to harmonise them verbally with the old cast-iron definitions of sovereignty and law, such modification destroys the original conception, while in the treatment of corporate life there arise serious practical dangers. Our first aim, then, must be to endeavour to induce men by persuasion and all means morally legitimate to admit the positive right of societies to exist, and in this we shall follow the example which was the origin of civil freedom. In the seventeenth century it was not the isolated individual but the religious body, the sect with its passionate assertion of its own right to be, which finally won toleration from the State. By himself apart from religious discords the individual would have secured no freedom. The orgy of State-autocracy which set in with the Renaissance and was developed by the Reformation would have gone on unchecked, as, indeed, it did in those States like France or the German principalities in which uniformity in religion was enforced. It was the competing claims of religious bodies, and the inability of any single one to destroy the others, which finally secured liberty. The rights of man were their recognition of the sense of his duties towards God. Political liberty is the fruit of ecclesiastical animosities.

Now, however, we are but at the threshold of our task. Once it has been realised as a problem of universal importance, a matter which concerns not clerical privilege but the very idea of corporate society, and involving the whole problem of the true nature alike of the State and the persons natural and juristic of which it is composed, we shall see that we are faced by further questions as to our duty as citizens and the limits which this freedom now claimed must place upon our efforts to influence the law of the land. Countless other questions will also arise, which I shall not do more than indicate. The right of the individual to liberty and self-development does not imply his right to do anything he pleases. Even so strong an individualist as Herbert Spencer was wont to guard the security of the liberty of each by reference to the equal liberty of all. If this be the case with individuals, it must still more plainly be so with all societies. For in the nature of things they are more powerful than individuals; the relative disinterestedness they claim from their members may, and often will, lead to methods and claims which cannot be justified; the higher their object, the greater danger there is of their outstepping the bounds of justice in their desire to promote it; and the greater need,

therefore, of government regulation and
control. Moreover, while the question of
the recognition of the individual citizen
is one that can be solved with no trouble,
the registration of a society and the deter-
mination of the marks which indicate its
full legal personality are more complex ; and
however strongly we may assert the natural-
ness of the corporate life, no one, I believe,
would deny the duty of the State to demand proper proofs that it is being formed
and supplied with duly constituted organs
of its unity ; while, further, it must clearly
be within the province of the State to prevent bodies of persons acting secretly, and
practically as corporations, in order to escape
the rightful government control. This, I
suppose, is half the difficulty of the trust
problem in America.   In regard to religion,
the State as " a power ordained by God "
ought not to allow men so to use the great
truth of freedom as to be false to the ends
of civil society.   No one, I suppose, would
now demand that the officers of corporate
bodies should not pay their debts, or claim
that the State may not use force to compel

them.[1]   Great as may be this freedom, we
have large tracts of life dependent on property and contract, which must come within
the control of the civil power.   Here, however, there may be one kind of exception.
Within any social group, if the members
are sufficiently loyal, there may grow up
all kinds of ties and arrangements which
could not be enforced at law, and yet are
practically restrictive.   For instance, at this
moment there is no restriction on publication except that provided by the law of
libel, yet the bulk of works published by
Roman Catholics have on them an *impri-
matur*.   This is a restriction not legally
enforceable, but dependent on the loyalty
to their own authorities of the members of
the Roman Church.   It would, however,
be a distinct invasion of the province of
that Church if the courts were to interfere

[1] "Sæculares judices qui, licet ipsis nulla competat
jurisdictio in hac parte, personas ecclesiasticas ad sol-
vendum debita, super quibus coram eis contra ipsas
earum exhibentur literæ vel prelationes aliæ inducun-
tur, damnapili præsumptione compellunt, a temeritate
hujusmodi per locorum ordinarios censura ecclesiastica
decernimus compescendos."— *Corpus Juris Canonici,
Sext* II. ii. 2.

with the excommunication of anyone on the ground that he had contravened this regulation. Even now between families and individuals a vast amount of arrangements go on which could not be legally enforced; nor will this ever cease to be needful. Except in a small and highly-undeveloped society, very many transactions must take place which depend for their validity on the character of men, and not on any legal instrument. Another instance is the matter of monastic vows. These are not now a legal obligation, but that they have a very practical effect is not doubtful. Certain exceptions do not prove the contrary, any more than the existence of criminals proves the law to be of none effect.

In regard to the matter of Churches, it is necessary to lay stress on the fact, that what we claim is freedom within the limits of civil society, and that we neither claim to be outside the law nor to exercise control over politics. For the whole question is prejudiced by recollections of the Middle Ages and the seventeenth century. Then, in one sense the Church was free, or seemed to be so; but, as I said last time, she was

still under the same notion of State autocracy as that of the ancient world, and
consequently she understood by freedom
supremacy: she demanded the proscription
of all those who did not accept her discipline: she identified citizenship with Churchmanship, and she claimed to dictate on
religious grounds the law and policy of the
State. Much of the prejudice against the
just claims of religious bodies arises from
the recollection of these facts, and the evils
of clerical immunities. Benefit of clergy
in the Middle Ages had more in its favour
than is often supposed; it served to mitigate
the barbarity of the ordinary law, and it set
limits to a royal authority which was striving by every means to become absolute.
Yet it did mean the definite withdrawal,
not of all justice, but of the protection
afforded by the King's Courts from all persons
injured by a clerk, and you know how
wide was the interpretation given to this.
Boniface VIII, at the close of the thirteenth century, went further, and denied
the right of the civil courts to enforce the
payment of debts by the clergy, and of the
State to tax them in the famous Bull *Clericis*

Laicos.   Boniface VIII went further than his predecessors, and definitely laid claim to a world monarchy in the Bull *Unam Sanctam.*[1]   This Bull was never an authoritative part of the *Corpus Juris Canonici;* but he did not do more than develop the claims inherent in the Canon Law and in the policy and utterances of such popes as Gregory VII, Innocent III, and Innocent IV.

It is perhaps well to say that we must acquit modern Rome of any such claim. We may all have our private opinion as to what would happen if she were once more in a position to make it ; and so far as can be judged from the case of Malta, the curia has no notion of allowing religious toleration, except where it cannot be helped. Be this as it may, it remains true that the theory of Ultramontanism, as laid down now, does not involve the absorption of the State in the Church, or the denial of civil society as a fact.   In the Encyclical *Immortale Dei*, issued in 1885 by Leo XIII,[2]

---

[1] It is one of the *Common Extravagants*, i. 8, 1.

[2] Printed in Denziger Enchiridion, 501–8.   " Ex iis autem Pontificum præscriptis illa omnino intelligi

Rome has developed for herself the doctrine that the Church is a perfect society set over against the other perfect society, the State; and not theoretically claiming more than liberty. This position is not identical with that here taken up, for the whole Roman tradition, which is based on the Civil and Canon Law, is steeped in the doctrine of fictitious personality. Yet at least it would pave the way for a truer notion of the relation of the State and the Church, than that possible to an age which in no way recognised the possibility of two societies quite distinct in nature and end, although composed of the same individuals. So far as I know, this conception of the two social persons was first put down by Bishop Warburton in his *Alliance between Church*

necesse est, ortum publicæ potestatis a Deo ipso non a multitudine repeti oportere; seditionum licentiam cum ratione pugnare. . . . Similiter intelligi debet, Ecclesiam societatem esse, non minus quam ipsam civitatem, *genere et jure perfectam;* neque debere qui summam imperii teneant, committere, ut sibi servire aut subesse Ecclesiam cogant aut minus esse sinant ad suas res agendas liberam, aut quicquam de ceteris juribus detrahant, quae in ipsam a Jesu Christi collata sunt" (503). The Encyclical goes on to assert the indifference of the forms of civil government.

and State, although here and there approaches had been made to it.[1] However this may be, there is no doubt that as soon as men were beginning to think of the State and the Church as each of them a *societas perfecta*, they were on the way to a more reasonable theory of the relations between the two, than that which was possible to the mind dominated by the antique idea of the unitary absolute State; whether that idea took the form predominantly political of Aristotle or Bodin, or the form predominantly theocratic of St. Augustine and Luther. In the discussions of the sixteenth century we begin to hear of this theory. Some of the Jesuits saw in it the means of defending the claims of the Church while supporting, at least in name, those of the State. The French royalists of the next century, like Barclay, developed

[1] Thorndike, for instance, in his *Right of the Church in a Christian State*, speaks clearly of the two societies as distinct, although composed of the same individuals. And this book had much influence. A similar claim to freedom is put out by Stillingfleet in his *Irenicum*. Neither, however, had reached the notion of persons; although, of course, the Presbyterians held the doctrine of the two societies. *Cf.* Appendix I.

it from the opposite standpoint. In this country the notion of the two kingdoms, which was substantially the same, was asserted by Thomas Cartwright, the leader of the Presbyterians, thereby provoking the astonished horror of Archbishop Whitgift, just as the ordinary doctrine of the Divine Right of the State was termed by the Jesuit Gretser *Machiavellistica ae Turcica*. In the nineteenth century the theory was worked out in detail by Camillo Tarquini in his *Juris Ecclesiastici Publici Institutiones*, and Palmieri in his *Tractatus de Romano Pontifice*. Both writers were Jesuits. Modern Ultramontanism, as developed by Eckstein, Möhler, and their friends, had something to do with this development. They saw the necessity of accepting the modern State, while as convinced and even passionate adherents of the Roman Church they re-claimed for the religious society a wider liberty than that allowed by anti-clericals. On this topic of the ultramontane scholars of the earlier nineteenth century, there is a very valuable early essay by Acton in the *Home and Foreign*

Review[1] for July 1863, out of which I quote the following description :

" The name of Ultramontanes was given in

[1] This has not been reprinted. There is an article, I believe, by Richard Simpson, on "The Individual, the Corporation, and the State," in the *Rambler* for May 1862, which sets forth the whole topic of this lecture with great insight and lucidity. I may cite the following passages :

"This theory of State absolutism supposes the State to be prior to all associations; it assumes that they must all ask its leave to exist before they have any right to be; and therefore that it has a continual right of inspection and supreme control over them. Hence it must follow that freedom is no general right, but a collection of liberties and immunities granted as concessions and compromises by the absolute power."

"The true aim of politics is to harmonise the three elements of the State—the free individual, the free corporation, and the free State—in such stability of equilibrium as shall leave to each the greatest amount of free scope that is possible without injury to others. There must be some combination of the absolute corporation, the absolute State, and the absolute person from the harmony of which the truest personal freedom arises. Taken singly by itself, each of these elements characterises a barbarous kind of existence. The absolute individual is found only in savage life; the absolute corporation in primitive patriarchal society; the absolute State in oriental despotisms."

One interest of the article arises from the perception by the writer of the point urged in the text, namely, the peculiar survival in English life of the true way of treating the relation of the three.

consequence of their advocacy of the freedom of the Church against the civil power; but the characteristic of their advocacy was, that they spoke not specially for the interests of religion, but on behalf of a general principle, which, while it asserted freedom for the Church, extended it likewise to other communities and institutions."

Now it is this recognition of the modern State which I desire to urge to-day. It may seem impertinent, if not absurd, to talk as though anyone was likely to ignore a fact, no less patent than the sun at noonday. But I think that the language sometimes used by supporters of the claims of the Church makes it less unnecessary than appears. We cannot eat our cake and have it. We cannot claim liberty for ourselves, while at the same time proposing to deny it to others. If we are to cry "hands off" to the civil power in regard to such matters as marriage, doctrine, ritual, or the conditions of communion inside the Church—and it is the necessary condition of a free religious society that it should regulate these matters—then we must give

up attempting to dictate the policy of the
State in regard to the whole mass of its
citizens. "Them that are without God
will judge." We are both citizens and
Churchmen. We have to try to look at
all these matters alike from the ecclesiastical
and from the civic standpoints. We have,
as members of the Church, the right and
duty to claim freedom within this society
for its own laws, ideals, and development;
as members of the State we have to think
and to vote for what is the wisest course
in a nation of which many of the Christians
refuse to submit to our discipline, and
many are not Christian at all. As citizens
we have no right or claim . to appeal
to motives or ideals specifically Christian,
or to lay down lines of policy which
have no meaning except from the standpoint of the Catholic Church. We must
recognise facts even where we do not like
them.

The cardinal fact which faces us to-day is
the religious heterogeneity of the modern
State. Toleration has not yet produced all
its fruits; perhaps it is nowhere quite complete. Still it is clear that the old ideal of

a uniform State religion has departed. The homogeneous polity of the Middle Ages and the seventeenth century has vanished like the shadow of a dream, although some of its results still survive. So far, indeed, as this ideal has vitality now, it takes the vague form of undenominational Christianity, which so many would like to establish in the schools, and a certain number of persons, including that amazing theological instructor, the *Spectator* newspaper, are definitely trying to make compulsory in the Church. That is the danger. You can go on preaching the notions which are ultimately those of a theocracy if you will, but so far as you are successful you cannot do more than establish the ideals of the man in the street. To the Catholic Church you will do no benefit, unless it be one to cause her to be persecuted; but you will not impossibly end by the establishment and endowment of the Pleasant Sunday Afternoon.

There is, indeed, one basis on which the Church as a Church can claim to dictate in matters of policy; but the basis is that of the discarded doctrine of religious uniformity with its corollary in persecution. If you are prepared to advocate that, by all means do so. Most people are not. Into this question of persecution I shall not enter; but it is well to consider it with critical eyes. Much inflated rhetoric is devoted to the topic of the wickedness of all persecution, very often by persons who are advocating measures which are essentially of that nature. Probably no one has reflected on the subject without finding that it is far more difficult to condemn persecution absolutely and in theory than the popular axiom would suggest.[1]

To begin with, we can most of us see the evils of the intellectual anarchy of our time, and the lack of all directing ideals in the Western World except those vulgarly materialistic. Is not all this the direct consequence of the religious toleration and the breaking down of the old doctrine of a homogeneous State? Or again, *Liberty*,

[1] *Cf.* Ritchie, *Natural Rights*, chap. viii., decides in favour of the use of the term " toleration," because it implies a grant of the community, and not an absolute unlimited right; *cf.* also the close of F. C. Montague, *The Limits of Individual Liberty;* and A. J. Balfour, *Essays.*

that characteristic work of John Stuart
Mill, gave men an ideal defence of toleration. But it was based on a distinction
which few now could maintain—that between acts purely self-regarding and those
which are not. Even if there are any acts
of the former nature, and it is very doubtful,
no religious body nor anyone else who has
ever persecuted but would deny that the
particular acts complained of were of that
kind. Perhaps this distinction would relieve us of the sheer persecution for the
good of the heretic's own soul, but it would
leave all others untouched. Persecution is
normally condemned on the ground that it
tampers with the individual conscience.
But the very conception of personality we
were developing in the last lecture seems to
militate against this view. If the individual
only comes to himself as part of a society,
his conscience is always partially social.
Why should not the society which has
made him what he is assert an authority
in the last resort coercive against him? It
may, and I think ought, to be said that the
authority of society is no more than a very
strong presumption; in the last resort the

individual must decide, and persecution denies this. But it may be doubted how far this will carry freedom to criticise existing institutions. Again, it is argued that you must punish acts and not opinions ; but the dissemination of ideas is an act, and under certain conditions it may have far more practical effect than an isolated deed. How different would the French Revolution have been if Rousseau had never written ? Does anyone suppose that the writers of the Bible were not producing an explosive, and one so violent that it is constantly re-exploding, very often to the intense amazement of those who profess to live by its precepts ? Or again, if you say that persecution is always wrong, *i.e.* the application to force to suppress any kind of opinion which the majority dislike, where are you to draw the line about actions ? Why should you prohibit public lotteries or gaming-tables, or require public-houses to be licensed, and so forth ? Because they affect the public health or physique, or may lead to breaches of the peace ? But so may a bad book. Or it may be said that the final objection to persecution is that it shuts the door to new

truth. This is virtually the old argument
of Gamaliel, and is probably the soundest.
The danger from false ideas is less than the
danger of obscurantism, and the consequent
stagnating effect on mind and morals. Yet
here again it may be argued, as was done
by Sir James Stephen, that such a practice
is at bottom sceptical. No one who is certain of his beliefs can admit the possibility
of a new and valuable discovery. But then
the same certainty may guarantee him
against the danger of being seduced from
his allegiance. But how about the mass
of men? Can we be sure of them? The
answer is that in the long run the religion
or belief that has established itself amid a
fire of criticism is purer than any other;
and that will be so even though its adherents are less numerous.[1] From the
Christian standpoint the great advantage
of toleration is that it elevates automatically
the life of the Church. At this moment
for every person we lose, who has dropped

---

[1] *Liberty, Equality, Fraternity.* The first chapter of
this book is a reply to John Stuart Mill, and is probably the ablest polemic in existence against Mill's
views on the liberty of thought and discussion.

a merely conventional religion owing to the greater liberty, we gain in the intensity of the religious life of those we keep. And we gain too by this very hostility. The advantage of toleration is that it acts automatically on the purity of religious bodies and the reality of their faith ; and, where complete, it produces a temper which, annealed in the fires of constant criticism, is analogous to that produced by persecutions in the earlier days of the Church. Mr. Benjamin Kidd has bidden us look forward to a time when all faith will meet with such a fire of criticism as has not before been known.[1] That fire is already kindled, and it purges out the weaklings. But all these topics, and they might be increased, serve only to show the difficulty of the problem.

What is clear to me is this fact. Even if some are unconvinced by the arguments for freedom, and look either backward or forward to a day when men shall be organised in society on a basis of religious unity, it must be plain that we do not live in such

[1] This is one of the most important arguments in his *Principles of Western Civilisation.*

an age; that there is nothing to be gained by pretending that we do; that whatever unity of opinion may underlie or come to underlie any probable polity, it will not be that body of doctrine which we know as the Catholic Creeds. What we have to face is a hurly-burly of competing opinions and strange moralities—"new thought" from the West, theosophies from the East, Pantheism all round us, Paganism revived, and unbelief in all its arrogance. All we can claim, all we can hope for, is freedom for ourselves as one society among many. It seems to me in a high degree dishonest, and even more imprudent, to go about and proclaim the rights of freedom and variety in the matter of education, if in other matters we seek to deny it. Liberty does not mean the right to punch the heads of those who disagree with you.

Let me take one or two instances. Let us take one burning question—that of marriage. It is confidently affirmed that, in a very brief space of time, we shall be in possession of proposals coming with all the authority of a Royal Commission to increase the facilities for divorce. Should such pro-

posals be made it will be our duty as
Churchmen to fight to the utmost for the
liberty to contract out, if I may so put it.
We need to have it perfectly clear—in a
way which not even the House of Lords
can repudiate—that any change in the law
of the land shall leave entirely unchanged
the freedom of the Church to insist on the
observance of the Christian law of marriage by all her communicating members,
and to exclude all who do not. But as
Churchmen we are not bound to go further.
We shall as citizens have our own opinions
as to what is for the national welfare; we
shall doubtless find many Positivists who
would agree with us that a really whole-
some standard of national life can be raised
only on a strict basis of monogamy; that
the sexual promiscuity, which is the real
aim of the opponents of marriage, is detri-
mental to the health, the comfort, and the
fighting morale and domestic happiness of the
people. But it is no more a matter strictly
for the Church as a body to lay down lines
of policy than it was for the Christians of
the Pagan Empire. The State, as it now is,
is composed not only of Christians, even if we

include all the sects, but of every variety of religion and no religion. One of the under-secretaries of His Majesty's Government is a person who varies his defence of Liberalism with public and repeated denials of the historic fact of our Lord's existence; and when he has spoken of Him, does so in terms of which the following is a specimen: "Some of the sayings attributed to Jesus have a relatively high moral value."[1] Such a man has every right to his place in the modern State; but what guidance can the law of the Christian Church be as to what shall be the wisest law to make in a society of which such people are the rulers? What may be the wisest rule for a nation so heterogeneously composed we cannot from the Christian standpoint positively say, and we shall probably differ greatly from one another. One consideration may be urged. The members of the Christian Church— even when supported by the sacraments and living in sincere faith in our Lord as the Redeemer—have throughout all ages been

[1] *Cf.* J. M. Robertson, *Pagan Christs : A Short History of Christianity.* The phrase quoted comes from *A Short History of Free Thought.*

retained with difficulty within these bonds, and breaches are not infrequent.   Is it very probable that these bonds will be found possible for those who repudiate the sanctions of Christian morality, who scorn the grace proffered to help the frailty of our nature, and for whom chastity is not even an ideal ?

And yet, even in regard to these matters, we hear of meetings of Churchmen repudiating all attempt to alter the law, or at least to widen it ; of demanding the repeal of the Act of 1857 and going back to the *status quo ante*, when divorce was a luxury for those who could afford to pay for a private Act of Parliament, and of demanding the enforcement upon a population no longer even nominally Christian of the whole series of tabooes and exclusions which Christians themselves find so difficult.   In other words, they are demanding quite plainly that the morality of the Church as such shall be imposed against their will upon those who owe her no allegiance.   Such demands seem to me tenable in theory only on the Puritan or mediæval notion of a State, and in practice as absurd as the proposal of

John Knox to punish adultery with death. What we ought as Churchmen to strain every nerve to do is to secure the repeal of that clause in the Act of 1857 which makes it obligatory on an incumbent to lend his church for the marriage of divorced persons, and to see to it that anything like similar provisions shall be absent from the new law, and also that every safeguard shall be left to us as a society for enforcing our own discipline. It will be hard enough to secure that much. The judgment of the House of Lords in the Bannister case has shown how words inserted for one purpose in a statute may be interpreted to mean precisely the opposite of what was intended. But if we are going to dissipate our energies in the attempt to impose our notions of morality by force on the entire population, we shall infallibly fail in the latter effort, and we shall have all the less likelihood of securing our own corporate freedom. I am not saying that every individual among us might not vote or write against such proposals; he may object to them as a change, or because they have this laxity in America, or for its effect on the children, or because

it is only a fad of a few of the rich, or because indissoluble marriage is affirmed by
the law of nature,[1] and so forth.   But he
ought not to be asked to oppose them on
grounds of loyalty to the Church ; and he
must remember that, as Dr. Sanday said,
the State is forced to act on principles of a
wise expediency, and to have regard to all
the groups of opinion within it.   On such
points opinions would infinitely vary, and
we should find allies or opponents in unexpected places.   What I object to being
asked to do is to vote one way or the other
on account of my Churchmanship in matters
which concern the life of millions of people,
many of whom have not the smallest intention of ever being Churchmen.   The Christian law is the law of Christians ; what may
be wise and right for a body of all faiths
and every fad is no matter for the Christian
Church to decide.

Other instances are ready to hand.   There
is the social question.   Moved by the intolerable wrongs and oppressions of our
industrial system, with its spectacle of

[1] This is the ground taken up by Mr. Lacey in his
Marriage in Church and State.

thousands of lives maimed and wasted and born with an evil environment, men are apt to claim that it is the duty of Christians as such to adopt some particular remedy, and to identify the Gospel with some definite organisation of society. That Churchmen ought to have a conscience in these matters is true; that it is the province of all who are teachers in the Church to awaken this conscience and to make their hearers far more uncomfortable than they are with the existing régime is certain. They ought to preach to them the duty of forming political or economic opinions with such regard to justice, such careful inquiry, and disinterested zeal for the whole people, and not merely a class, as they may. They may warn them against the danger of opposition to changes owing to the prejudices of their own environment or the fear of being less well off. They ought to preach, much more than they do, that a Christian ought to be prepared to forego sources of income or methods of business open to others, and to scrutinise the undertakings from which his own income is derived; to be considerate to employés, to servants of every kind; to be less extravagant in clothes or ornaments than those who are not Christians. Of this teaching we have all too little. The average layman of the comfortable class seems to have little notion that his standard ought to be, in any way, higher than that of his neighbours over the way who are not Christians; and his sons, and still more his daughters, have, for the most part, even less. Of course there are exceptions; but I am speaking of the ordinary churchgoer. But, whereas so much is needed here, too little is given. So far as many of those who are concerned with these matters go, an effort is made to indicate that he must, as a Christian, be in favour of this or that scheme, the Minority Report of the Poor Law for instance, or else his attention is directed to vast schemes of social reorganisation which he can do little to forward, and, in any case, are unlikely to be realised, save in a far future. I do not say that he should not be directed to consider the evils of the capitalist system or bidden to seek a solution. I wish our congregations were roused to this more and more. But I do not think any policy ought to be forwarded by the Church as a corporate society, and imposed in its name in a State of which Churchmanship has no longer anything to do with the qualifications of a citizen. Those who take their ethical ideas from Nietzsche or their practice from Gabriele d'Annunzio, are hardly likely to be in favour of Christian solutions; and they have every whit as much a place in the State as you or I. The evils of capitalism are " gross, open, huge as mountains," and the oppression of the poor cries to heaven; what we need to persuade Church people is of their own duty in regard to their own wealth and the means of getting it. Consider how vast would be the change if every regular communicant in the Church of England—we will omit the rest for the moment—were sincerely to embrace the maxim of St. Paul, that " having food and raiment we ought therewith to be content," and, without descending from the legitimate expenses of his station, were for himself or his children to give up thinking of a large income as the one desideratum; were to cease judging occupations at their cash value; were to limit himself severely in the matter of motor-cars, hotels, theatres, and clothes for his daughters and to give the rest in charity, and to spend time saved from amusements in some form of social work. If those who have a competence, whether earned or inherited, were no longer to be driven by the ceaseless desire for more and ambition for their children, there would be a revolution in the face of things, and many of our problems would solve themselves. So much energy would be set free for worthy objects that the tone of the nation and social life would speedily be raised. Now, I do not see how such things can be preached to an agnostic or a hedonist ; they are absurd on his principles. But they ought not only to be preached but practised by all communicant members of the Christian Church. If in no age can we expect perfection in these matters, and must always allow for a fringe of those of lower standard, the quiet worldliness of many and the self-complacent enjoyment of position by really devout Christians are perhaps the peculiar evil of the Church of England.

What I am anxious to emphasize is that,

I

primarily, the business of Christians is with the moral standard of their own society and with themselves as its members. The raising of that will gradually bring about the elevation of the great mass of those who do not belong to it. So long as Churchmen do not see, except in a few matters, such as Sunday observance and sexual morality, any real reason why they should have any higher standard than the world at large, so long is the Christian Church failing in its mission. And the attempt to confuse this object with that of securing a better social organisation to be imposed by law on the whole nation seems to me likely to enfeeble the former without ultimately strengthening the latter. We want an enormously heightened public opinion within the Church, and then it is bound to affect the world at large. That is what happened in the early days of the Church. Any attempt to impose the opposite doctrine seems to me partly to be a survival from the régime of the seventeenth century, and from the theocratic ideals which Puritans and Carolines alike inherited from the Middle Ages; and partly due to the definite effort to establish an all-embracing humanitarian Church-State, which would ultimately mean the destruction of all freedom in religious bodies. For the unitary doctrine of the State leads only, in very rare instances, to the establishment of the claims of the Church (which from this standpoint are always illegitimate), and then they only take the form of supremacy. In nine cases out of ten it means the secularising of the Church, and the dominance of Erastianism. We can see this at the present moment. The attempt to force the Church law of marriage on all, the refusal to let the State go her own way provided we can go ours, has led, as a matter of fact, to the strangest indiscretions. Language is sometimes used which appears to mean that the House of Commons as at present constituted is the true interpreter of the words of our Lord about adultery. A recent book by the Dean of Ripon on *Natural Christianity* shows a desire to admit all persons to its privileges on the ground of nationality apart from any question of religion. Others raise the cry of sectarianism whenever any attempt is made to enforce a rule of the

Church, oblivious of the fact that unless you definitely enforce religious belief, the Christian Church, however broadly defined, can be only a sect, a part of the modern nation. Sectarianism, in the sense in which it is condemned by Canon Hensley Henson, the Dean of Ripon, or the Editor of the *Spectator*, is not the evil fruit of High Churchmanship; it is the result of the principle of toleration. Where all beliefs are held, those who profess any one can be no more than a part, and thus unity in belief will ultimately make them a society, *i.e.* a sect. Even if you reduce Christianity to a Unitarian Modernism, Christians will still be distinct from those who have no faith in the other world; and that difference will enormously differentiate their whole life and standards of value. Even if you go further, and identify Christianity with a vague humanitarianism, independent of faith or unbelief in God, still there will be those who do not hold it. For instance, the followers of Nietzsche would certainly have been excluded from any such body; and then even a Positivist Christianity, with the motto of kindness as its one maxim, would have to be ultimately separated off, *i.e.* a sect in a world where no restriction is laid upon opinion.

We cannot escape sectarianism even by sacrificing the creeds; still less by attempting a wholly unreal identification of the Church with the nation, an identification which had ceased to represent all the facts even in the time of Hooker, and has been becoming less true ever since. Neither, on the other hand, in such a world can you without disaster attempt to impose the standards of the Church on the whole mass of your countrymen, except in so far as they still rule in some matters on other grounds. Every attempt to raise the code of the nation to that of the Church leads, if unsuccessful, to an attempt to lower the code of the Church to that of the world, because it proceeds from a notion that at bottom the two are identical. Thus if the lax party gets the upper hand it will compel the Church to conform to its standards, an attempt which is being made on all hands just now. The two societies are distinct— distinct in origin, in aim, and (if you have toleration) in personnel. The smaller is never likely, as things are, to control the larger. If she attempt to do so she will be beaten, and in the process be like to lose her own freedom. The Puritans attempted to raise the nation to their own notions of a high morality. The consequence was seen after the Restoration. It is the essence of the Church to be different from the world, and her mission to proclaim that difference. Whenever men try to sanctify the world by raising it to the level of the Church, they commonly succeed only in lowering the life of the Church to accommodate it to the practice of the world. The two centuries which began with Pope Boniface VIII ended with Alexander VI.

LECTURE IV

ULTRAMONTANISM

IT remains to consider the development within the Church of a theory analogous to that which we have been combating in the State. From a human standpoint it is the final and fatal objection to the Roman claims that they are inextricably bound up with this false theory of the omnipotent sovereign.

" The ghost of the Roman Empire sitting crowned on its grave " was the name given to the Papacy by Thomas Hobbes. It is this aspect alone of the Roman Church which I wish you to consider.

In this regard, the development of the *Corpus Juris Canonici*, with the principles that underlie it, has merely meant the taking over from the *Corpus Juris Civilis* of the conception of the sovereign power of the Emperor, and its transference to the Pope. The doctrine of the *plenitudo potestatis*, of which we hear in all their writing, is purely the Roman theory of sovereignty vested in the Pope. The differences are all in favour of the Papal autocracy. The Emperor received his power by the grant of the people, and according to some theories they may withdraw what has been granted. By this means a direct path was opened to Rousseau's doctrines. The Pope has received his power directly from God, and is therefore in no way amenable (unless conceivably in the case of heresy). The Church is thus conceived merely as a State on the antique model, with all power centred in the Pope or derived from him, and no jurisdiction nor any rights existing except expressly or tacitly by his delegation. The ultramontane theory of the Episcopate, and even of the Apostolate, while it does not claim for the Pope the sole power of conferring the sacred orders, derives every kind of episcopal jurisdiction from him, and allows for local differences only by use of subterfuges dear to the abstract theorists of sovereignty. Let me quote a passage from the *Sext*. " Licet

Romanus Pontifex, qui jura omnia in scrinio pectoris sui censetur habere, constitutionem condendo posteriorem, priorem quamvis de ipsa mentionem non faciat, revocare noscatur; quia tamen locorum specialium et personarum singularium consuetudines et statuta, quum sint facta et in facto consistant potest probabiliter ignorare; ipsis dum tamen sint rationabilia, per constitutionem a se noviter editam nisi expresse caveatur in ipsa, non intelligitur in aliquo derogare."

Here, then, is the definite application to the Pope of the civilian doctrine of the Emperor as the source of all law; while the theory of his being ignorant of fact is a transparent dodge, through which it was possible to allow local liberties in practice, while denying them in theory. The same quibble was used by the great Italian civilian, Bartolus, a little later on to account for the practical freedom of the Italian City-State, while preserving the theoretic claims of imperialism; which in one place he declares it probably heresy to question. Extended to civil affairs this claim is clearly the denial of all freedom to the secular power. Under the theory of the single society, which, as we have seen in the previous lecture, dominated the Middle Ages, it was not possible to claim such supreme power for the Pope, without subjecting to him all the princes. The doctrine of the two swords is a picturesque symbol of this. The two swords which the disciples offered to our Lord in the garden typify the spiritual and the civil power respectively; both are to be used for the Church in the sense of the hierarchy, the spiritual directly and the temporal indirectly. Thus it can be said definitely by the clerical protagonist in the late mediæval dialogue the *Somnium Viridarii*, which sets out all the stock arguments on either side, that in the last resort *omnia jura civilia sunt canonica*, and writers like Augustinus Triumphus, or a little later Bozius, would deliberately maintain that the Pope was "king of kings and lord of lords," and that the kingdoms were the *stipendia* to their rulers for doing the dirty work of the Church. This doctrine, however, was never universal; an indirect power, as asserted by Bellarmine in the controversies of the sixteenth century, was the more usual form. This did allow a relative independence and a real existence to the State, and it paved the way for the doctrine of the two societies, each complete in itself, so that the Church with the Pope at its head is *genere et jure perfecta*, and will allow the State to go its own way provided it leaves the Church internal liberty.

It is not with the political and external aspects of the ultramontane claim that we are to-day concerned, although it was needful to point out how inevitably these claims grow up out of the belief that the Pope is Lord of the Church by Divine right, and has a *plenitudo potestatis.* All we need to do is to consider something of the historic origin and juristic nature of these claims within the Church as the society of baptized believers, after making abstraction of the numerous conflicts they brought about with the secular power. Furthermore, the strictly theological problem is one into which we cannot enter. Neither the actual development of the Papal theory out of the antique State and the civil law, nor the fundamental fallacy of this doctrine of illimitable sovereignty, have any real bearing on the argument from Divine right. If our Lord instituted St. Peter Prince of the Apostles in such a way that all their jurisdiction is derived from St. Peter either tacitly or expressly, and if from him downwards all jurisdictions have been concentrated in the Bishop of Rome, it is clear that no argument concerning the influence of the civilian forms of thought will destroy that fact. If the Petrine texts have the meaning which Ultramontanes say they have, *cadit quæstio.* All I am concerned to do is to point out, that as a matter of historic fact the phenomenon of the Papacy appears in the world as the residuary legatee of the Roman Empire, and that as a matter of polity the Church on the ultramontane theory suffers from all the defects which attach to the State, when conceived in this abstract fashion.

Apart, then, from this direct topic of the Petrine texts, the arguments by which this concentration of power in a single person are justified, are precisely the same as those used in civil matters. There must be unity

in the society, or it ceases to be one; to be
a single society, a single head, if not essential, is most convenient; the psychological
struggles inside the mind of a monarch are
less likely to cause division than the conflicts
within a governing assembly. The bees and
geese have autocrats. Peace, the very end
of all polity, and especially Church polity,
is unthinkable without a power absolutely
sovereign. The power of dispensing laws—
and we know the Pope has that—implies a
complete authority over them. Earthly rule
must be a copy of the heavenly; God is a
single individual ruling as an autocrat; so
must be the Pope. It is noteworthy that
this doctrine of sovereignty leads in the long
run to false views of God, no less than of
the State; in order to assert it freely, man's
liberty has to be denied. If you will take
the trouble to glance either through Calvin's
Institutes or Luther's *De Servo Arbitrio*,
you will see that in both cases the denial
of freedom to man comes, not like that of
modern determinism from an analysis of
human psychology, but from a determina-
tion to preserve God's omnipotence at all
costs, and a deductive argument from the

doctrine of the unity and freedom of the Divine autocrat. The fault of the Calvinist theology is that its one governing principle on which all else lies is the absolute sovereignty of God; instead of starting from the love of God and working on to the notions of His government and the self-limitation involved alike in the incarnation and the creating of free beings, Calvin starts from the notion of God as a *princeps legibus solutus*, who has *omnia jura in scrinio pectoris sui*, and deduces from thence the whole hideous spectacle of predestined evil and unavoidable damnation. If this view were true, and it is still widely credited, the blasphemy of Omar could be justified:

"Oh! Thou who did the clay of baser metal make,
    And even with Paradise devise the snake:
    For all the sin wherewith the face of earth
    Is blacken'd—man's forgiveness give—and take!"

The civilian conception of Papal sovereignty, to give things their true names, did not establish itself without a struggle. Latent for a time in the very fact of the Pope as living at the centre of the ancient world, it developed itself out of the need of organising and ruling the child races of the conquering barbarians. The revival of Roman Law in the University of Bologna, coupled with the growing powers of the Popes, caused the interpreters of Papal decisions to desiderate a body of scientific doctrine like the great *Corpus;* with this view Gratian published in 1139 his famous *Decretum,* or the *Concordia Discordantium Canonum.* This book is merely a private work which attempts to remodel the form of the existing law as it was being administered, and to assimilate it to the scientific method of the civilians. Then, a century later, Pope Gregory IX (1234) promulgated to the University of Bologna the five books of Papal decisions which had been arranged by Raymond of Pennaforte. This is the *Decretale,* and is statute law. At the end of the same century the last of the truly mediæval Popes, the great canonist and fighter, Boniface VIII, issued a further book (also by a Bull to the University of Bologna), which, as adding one to the five books already known, is called the *Sext.* Other collections of later date are the *Clementine* and *Johannine Extravagants*

and the *Common Extravagants*. These,
however, are merely collections, and are not
authoritative. For instance, the Bull *Unam
Sanctam* has never been officially part of the
law of the Roman Church. It is doubtful
whether such a Pope as Leo X would have
been willing to appeal to its principles.
I must apologise for stating plain and
well-known facts, which will be more than
familiar to many here ; but I wish to point
out that, alike in form and contact, these
various collections witness to a *crescendo* of
Papal claims, and to a growing hardening of
the full ultramontane theory of the Papacy.
You may see, if you will, the whole doctrine
latent in the letters of Hildebrand, and
deny that there is any true development.
Certainly he would not have disowned the
claims made by Boniface VIII, or, later on,
by John XXII. Yet the latter positively
claimed far more than Gregory VII, or even
Innocent III, had ever dreamed of—*e.g.*
to have the administration of the Empire
during a vacancy, while the theocratic
and prophetic cast of Hildebrand's mind
caused him to lay stress rather on the Scrip-
tural and Divine nature of his claims than

on a theory which is at bottom juristic and political.

We have seen that the Papal theory was developed on the lines of canonists trained in civil law; for a long while every canonist was to some extent a civilian, and when John of Salisbury, desiring to turn Becket on to more devotional lines, asks him what real good for souls the study of the canons or the laws has ever done, he alludes to the fact that a student of the canons would certainly also be one of the civil law of Rome. It is also true that the great expression of anti-Papal doctrine owed much to theories developed by writers who were primarily secularists. In the great fourteenth-century conflict between John XXII and Louis of Bavaria, not only our own William of Ockham in his great *Dialogue* and other works, but also Marsilius of Padua in the *Defensor Pacis*, developed a theory of representative government. By this time, moreover, feudalism had developed into the mediæval system of estates, and the very definite notions of a mixed or limited monarchy, that triumphed in this country in the

K

revolution of 1399, which overthrew Richard II.

Towards the close of the fourteenth century the Church was in the throes of the great schism. Until this was closed by the Council of Constance in 1414, *i.e.* for a period of forty years, the thoughts of all politically minded ecclesiastics were diverted from the question of the two powers to the consideration of the constitution of the hierarchical government of the Church. In their necessity they were driven to postulate sovereignty for the whole of the faithful, as against the Papal monarchy ; to claim for the councils the powers of supremacy and deposition ; and to transfer that constitutionalism, which was the crown of mediæval life, from the secular to the spiritual authority. In other words, the Conciliar movement, more especially as it flowers in the Whiggism of Gerson and the constructive federalism of Nicolas of Cues in the *De Concordantia Catholica*, is a definite assertion within the Church of the needs of a balanced constitution, of what men in a later age were to call a mixed or limited monarchy. Also, it was an assertion of the national

spirit against mere cosmopolitan central-
isation. To the Conciliar movement of the
fifteenth century and to its great, though
not recognised leaders, all of us must recur
who have regard at once to the historic
claims of the episcopate, the great tradition
of the whole Catholic Church, and at the
same time are anxious to see the movement
constitutional and federalistic, with due regard paid to real life of the parts. That
movement, however, failed. With the
triumph of the Papacy began the new
absolutism. We must not be misled, as
too many are, by English history. Beginning with the Renaissance, gathering
increased speed and force from the momen-
tum of the Reform movement, absolutism
developed itself with amazing strength
throughout the whole of Western Europe,
until it was checked by the American
Revolt and the French Revolution. England and Holland are the two exceptions
to prove the rule. Indeed English history
is never rightly understood by those who
treat constitutionalism as its natural and
inevitable issue. To the Tudor kings and
the Stuart statesmen monarchy always

seemed the natural and proper development for a country which was to be *dans le mouvement* ; freedom, the rights of Parliament, the safeguards of the Courts were regarded as things obsolete, mediæval, inefficient, clogs on the great wheels of State and invasions of its *arcana.* This process, or rather this state of mind, which is always oblivious of individual rights as being *bourgeois* and scorns the smaller forms of communal existence as parochial, in the long run was fatal to all the free life of corporations. We can see hints of it in the reigns of Charles II and James II. Its complete victory in the German principalities, and the destruction of the old guild life and all the little sanctities and realities of local and provincial loyalty, can be read in the second volume of Dr. Gierke's great work.

But the most important landmark which heralded all the rest is the victory of Pope Eugenius IV over the Council of Basel, which, after sitting nominally for eighteen years, dissolved itself in 1449. This victory was consolidated by Nicholas V and Pius II, who in his Bull *Execrabilis* forbade any-

one to appeal to a general council on pain
of excommunication, on the ground that it
was a body which might never come into
being.   The absolutism of the Papacy was
defended by writers like John of Torque-
mada (not the Inquisitor).   From that time
all the rest of the Papal developments were
the natural issue.   The federalism and
independent life of the Teuton fellowship
world was finally vanquished.   When it
asserted itself again, it was in a more violent
form, and that element was expelled; and
we hasten on to the time when a Pope
could say in all seriousness *La tradizione
son io.*   Infallibility is a necessary corollary
of this theory of jurisdiction.   If the whole
government of a Church believed to exist
by Divine right is vested in one man, not
as administrator but as lord; then, since
the Church is religious life, his infallibility
is a logical corollary.   Practically, however,
in this regard, of far greater significance is
the denial of all living reality to any other
person or body within the Church.   The
apotheosis of the Pope has destroyed Episco-
pacy as a serious force, while not even in
theory has the layman any right beyond

obedience. The cardinal error of the Encyclical *Pascendi* is its treatment of the laity as purely passive, the denial to them of any true place in the Church. For its condemnation of the extremer modernism much is to be said. But its attitude to the laity is only to be paralleled by the dictum of the eighteenth-century prelate, that the mass of the people have nothing to do with the law except to obey it. Moreover, this dictum, however cynical, is practically true in all the modern huge States, except where there is a strong development of local and corporate societies, and real self-government. The mere fact of a system of so-called representatives will not secure freedom. We have in fact reached a point in the history of the Church when, so far as his own communion goes, the Pope could say *L'Eglise c'est moi* with far more complete truth than Louis XIV could have said it of the State.[1]

True, all this concerns jurisdiction and sovereign power rather than purely spiritual things, and in the matter of conferring

[1] Of course he did not say it. We owe the story to Voltaire.

sacred orders the Pope has no more power than the humblest bishop, any more than in that of celebrating the sacrament a bishop differs from a priest. For all that, it is not easy to understand how anyone could have thought possible another decision, than that which condemned Anglican Orders, as coming from an authority imbued with the ultramontane principles. How could the intention be right, if it were an intention to ordain men as ministers of a body the jurisdiction of which the Pope does not recognise? For in ultramontane theory the Pope is omnipresent, and every bishop, every priest even, is only the Pope's delegate, just as every police-court magistrate represents "His Majesty the King, his crown and dignity." From the ultramontane standpoint, to suggest that a parish or province or even a national Church could exist as such apart from the fountain of all its life, would be like saying that you would have a legal jurisdiction in any royal country apart from the king of it.

Even, however, if the matter of orders were granted, we should be in little better case. For we should be an unorganised

mass, and our bishops would have no jurisdiction. This must be so, if the Pope is
the source of legal right in the Church.
The question about Rome is at the bottom
of the question as to whether the Church
is a State in the antique Græco-Roman
sense, with all power concentrated at the
centre, and every form of independent life,
corporate or individual, denied—such *simul-
acra* of it as exist being allowed only at the
permission, tacit or express, of the sovereign
Pontiff. The sense in which the Pope is
the Church on the modern ultramontane
theory is probably more, not less profound,
than most English folk imagine. Of course
I am speaking of theory. In practice, a
doctrine so deeply at variance with the facts
of life is less dangerous than appears. For
human nature always goes on, even if you
deny that it exists (precisely as determinists
in theory have to act and judge as though
freedom were a fact), and the actual Roman
communion, made up of many peoples,
nations, and languages, containing innumerable guilds and societies, and countless
orders and fellowships, and embracing
churches of the most diverse intellectual

and emotional climate stretching in un-
broken continuity through all the centuries
—that body has within her exhaustless
springs of beauty, and flowers of a rich
and overflowing piety ; she exhales from
her million churches a perfume as of the
prayers of the saints throughout the ages,
and still contains such springs of love and
sacrifice, that no stone ought to be cast
at her.   Also, to a large extent, she
remains the Church of the poor.   Ultramontanism as a juristic and social doctrine
is what we combat—not the actual Catholic
life of Spanish or Irish or Bavarian Christians.
From all of them we have more to learn
than we like to think.   Yet it remains the
case that the Roman theory is false, and
for precisely the same reason that the
doctrine of the unrestrained omnipotence
of the State is false.   It is not congruous
with the facts of life.   It attempts to ignore
the fact that the force of State action is a
synthesis of living wills, no mere logical
theory deduced from the notion of unity.
However, all this is only what we have
been already discussing.   What is worth
adding is this.   A doctrine which denies

reality and all self-developing life to the parts of the body politic is in religion yet more disastrous than in civil society, because in the long run it must destroy the springs of spiritual life in the individual conscience. Wherever blind obedience is preached, there is danger of moral corruption. Englishmen, however, would do well to remember that the present fashion is to preach this doctrine of blind obedience, not to an infallible Church or a gilded autocrat, but to a non-representative Parliament and a jerrymandering administration. Whether, however, the doctrine of omnipotence be proclaimed in Church or State, whether it take the form of monarchy by Divine right or the sovereignty of the people, always and everywhere this doctrine is false; for whether or no men can frame a logical theory to express the fact, the great fact at the root of all human society is that man is a person, a spiritual being; and that no power—not even a religious society—is absolute, but in the last resort his allegiance to his own conscience is final. In regard, moreover, to the Church, we cannot often enough repeat that the Church of the future must be a laymen's Church (although it still must have its priesthood), that is, the great democracy of God's servants and Christ's brethren, and no exclusive or illimitable power into which they may not look.

Further, I think we have good grounds for attributing to the ultramontane Papacy the character of a transient historical phenomenon, resulting from the special circumstances of the development of Western Europe. On a view of history it is seen that the Papacy is a growth of the human conditions of the Roman Empire and the principles inherent in the *Corpus Juris Civilis*. It is really a very local, in a sense provincial, institution as compared with Christendom as a whole. Doubtless that is a view of Christianity, as a fact in universal history, taken by many nowadays; but while it is not hard to show grounds for holding that the Catholic Church is the central thing in the spiritual history of mankind, it is not so easy with the actual fact before us of the Eastern Churches and other communions, to argue that the same can be true of the ultra-legalist doctrine of the omnipotent autocracy concentrated at Rome. What is certain is that in this view the condemnation of the English Church as a corporate society, a true part of the whole, is inevitable, and it is not arbitrary. It proceeds directly from the principle of denying all life to the parts and provinces of the Church, except that which is derived from the centre—and assuming Rome to be the centre.

In order to justify the English Church now and since the Reformation, you have to establish two things: (1) that the parts, in this case a nation, or if you will the two provinces, have such inherent powers of life and self-development, that the breach with the Papacy did not affect them vitally; (2) that what they did or suffered was not of such a nature as to cut these parts off from that stream of universal communal life we call the Catholic Church. For that purpose it is needful to reassert the principles set out in the fifteenth century at Constance and at Basel.

The problem is concerned with the nature of authority in the Church and with the transmission of that communal life. In controversy the form which this argument

has taken has been largely that of a discussion on the true interpretation of the
Petrine texts. With an iteration almost
wearisome the Conciliar party assert that
the commission to St. Peter was a commission to the whole Church; that the
Papal power is only representative; that he
is not *dominus* but *minister;* that he may
be restrained, and even deposed, as he was.
I think some went so far as to say that the
Papacy might be abolished, if the Church
saw fit, for *orbis major urbe.* None of the
Conciliar writers could dispute that the
actual administrative power rested in the
Pope, although many wished to curtail it
and to devise a definite system of constitutional government. Still, the Pope's
authority is merely that of the mouth-
piece; the real authority is that which
exists diffusively in the whole *communitas
fidelium.*

Similar is the contention of Bossuet in
his *Defensio Cleri Gallicani* at the close of
the seventeenth century. Everywhere the
appeal is to universal consent. Even from
the canonist and ultramontane side many
would be found to argue that law to be

valid needs not only Papal promulgation but also general acceptance. Thus a custom of disregarding law, if well established, could of itself abrogate it. The true problem then is that concerning the nature of authority in a society.

Now authority may sometimes come from above; and be purely external, like that of a master over his slave, or a general over his army. But, as a matter of fact, in any society authority arises in a more natural manner than this, and is more subtle. It is more often instinctive and inarticulate, what we call tone or atmosphere, than categorical and legislative. It arises from that total complex of influences, personal, historical, spiritual, moral, æsthetic, which are greater than the individual, which mould men's minds and wills even when they are unaware of it—to which the most rebellious anarchist pays toll, even by talking in the same language. Take an English public school; there assuredly there is authority. But you will not tell me that it is merely the will of the headmaster, even though technically he, as " Leviathan," might forbid every other form of it.

Neither again is it in the assistant-masters, nor in the prefects; nor in all these together. It is something far deeper than the will of any official or of a corporate body of officials; and it is potent over them, no less than over their subjects. It is surely the general expression of the communal life in the school, which goes on from generation to generation, which is being silently moulded every day and year, which in the most conservative of societies is always slightly changing, which includes in its sphere all the written rules and stated commands, all the personal qualities of past and present officials; and not only theirs, but that of every single member of the society. The new boy, to whom it seems at first purely external, is yet always a part of this very authority which he obeys, and will have his own effect, slight or weighty, on the total result. Probably it is best expressed by the term of Rousseau, *The General Will;* and like Rousseau we must insist that every individual has and must have by the nature of things his share in forming that General Will, even though at any moment it may go entirely against his own judgment, except the one desire to continue a member of the society. Authority is in fact the expression of the social nature of man, and the true character of personality. Its only true antithesis is a pure individualism which springs in thought from the barest rationalism, and in politics leads to anarchy. In so far as it permits a political or ecclesiastical society, such individualism can do so only on the grounds of expediency, and the most legalist form of the doctrine of a social contract.

The difficulties in this latter have been well summed up by Mr. Arthur Balfour in what is perhaps the most valuable chapter in *The Foundations of Belief*. After setting out the pure individualist and rationalist theory, he goes on : " Sentiments like these are among the commonplaces of political and social philosophy ; yet, looked at scientifically, they seem to me to be not merely erroneous, but absurd. Suppose for a moment a community of which each member should deliberately set himself to the task of throwing off so far as possible all prejudices due to education ; where each should con-

sider it his duty critically to examine the
grounds whereon rest every positive enact-
ment and every moral precept which he has
been accustomed to obey; to dissect all the
great loyalties which make social life possible,
and all the minor conventions which help
to make it easy; and to weigh out with scru-
pulous precision the exact degree of assent
which in each particular case the results of
this process might seem to justify. To say
that such a community, if it acted upon the
opinions thus arrived at, would stand but a
poor chance in the struggle for existence is
to say far too little. It could never even
begin to be; and if by a miracle it was
created, it would without doubt immediately resolve itself into its constituent
elements."

It is nearly twenty years since these
words were written, and the movement of
which M. Bergson is the most eminent representative is giving to Mr. Balfour's whole
view a wider support than seemed at first
likely. Yet, on the other side, the demand
for a universal criticism, beginning with the
cradle, is louder than ever; and a Cambridge Regius Professor of History has gone

L

so far as to say that the great command of
the future is yet to be, "Children distrust
your parents."[1]

But, though authority is thus necessary,
it is not merely something external or super-
imposed, but is part of the personality of the
person who submits to it. This is so even
with religious authority. In its barest form,
the discipleship of Christ, there must ever
be present an element of authority. He is
Master, and that must mean that the
disciple, having on general grounds sub-
mitted to His Lordship, must be prepared
to follow Him where he knows not, and to
act in advance of what his own individual
reason can tell him at the moment. Yet,
at the same time, it is partly the disciple's
choice that makes him one ; the relation is
mutual, and so it must be if the disciple is
to interpret the commands of his leader. So
it always is with the most elaborate system.
The creed of Pope Pius V may unite all
members of the Roman communion, but
what each one means by it he must decide
for himself; how it bears on his total self;

[1] J. B. Bury, *History of Freedom of Thought*, last
paragraph.

what content he gives to many of its notions; what grounds he has for adhering to this or that individual statement. Even if he takes the whole merely on the authority of the Church, he does so as being himself one of its members, and his own life and thought will have some bearing, however slight, in determining for others what the creed implies and the grounds of allegiance. One thing, however, is clear from what we have said, that creeds and formularies are not to be considered *in vacuo*— debated as lists of propositions, and judged externally. They are the intellectual expression of the total life of the Church, and have their meaning in reference to the controversies which evoked them. At moments when the root fact, the supernatural character of the Christian life, was threatened, there flashed out from the communal consciousness, the true authority, those expressions of faith designed to guard, and, as a fact, effectively guarding, that supernatural character.

The Bishops at Nicæa spoke as witnesses in the crisis of Arianism : they set forth the essence of that Christian life which they all shared; not what it should be, but what it was. But this was not all. In the diffusive consent of the whole Christian body, no less than in the organic expression of the Council, lies the true authority of the creed, and of the whole law or customs, of the Church. We must not separate the two in thinking of the final result. This point and the whole topic of the communal consciousness of the Church is admirably set out in the famous but ill-starred essay by Newman, " On Consulting the Faithful," published in the *Rambler* in 1858. Perhaps I may cite from him two passages. "First, I will set down the various ways in which theologians put before us the bearing of the consent of the faithful upon the manifestation of the tradition of the Church. Its concensus is to be regarded: (1) As a testimony to the apostolical dogma ; (2) *as a sort of instinct, or φρόνημα, deep in the bosom of the mystical body of Christ ;* (3) as a direction of the Holy Ghost ; (4) as an answer to its prayer ; (5) as a jealousy of error which it at once feels as a scandal." " I think certainly that the *Ecclesia docens* is more happy when she has such enthusiastic partisans about her, as are here represented, than when she cuts off the faithful from the study of her divine doctrines and the sympathy of her divine contemplations, and requires from them a *fides implicita* in her word, which in the educated classes will terminate in indifference and in the poorer in superstition." I take it that now, as compared with the years 1872 or 1873, a Roman controversialist would be justified in appealing to this same principle, as giving to the Vatican definitions an authority which they had not when originally proclaimed.

However that may be, there can be no doubt that on the ultramontane theory all authority is gathered at the centre and not merely administered there; and that the Church lives by virtue of what can be derived from the Pope. Now the theory on which the English Church (and ultimately the same is true of the Gallican view), bases its doctrine is the direct opposite of this. The authority of the Church is not an abstract doctrine deduced from the notion of unity; but it is a synthesis of all the living parts of the Church. True, a connection exists between them, or one could not talk of the Catholic Church; but just as in St. Paul's time the Catholic Church was present equally in the Churches of Ephesus, or Corinth, or Rome, or Antioch, as it was in Jerusalem at the centre; so now on our view the life of the Church is real in every nation, in every province, in every diocese, and does not exist by grace of the Pope. Any universal constitution to which we might approach, would be ultimately of the federalist type; and so long as the sacraments are maintained, this life is not destroyed either by the fact of schism, very rarely a unilateral offence, or by the curtailment of rites in themselves laudable. We can assert the Catholicity of the Church of England—*universitas quædam*, as Lyndwood calls her—without denying that in many ways her life has been impoverished, more especially in those which have regard to the Communion of Saints. Too little indeed have men drunk at the deep wells of Catholic devotion; too callous are many of them still to that clothing "all glorious within," which adorns as with wrought gold "the King's daughter," the bride of Christ. Too sadly have they neg-

lected the rich treasures of the great
human-divine life we call the Church, and
despised its long roll of heroes, and turned
in scorn from its diadem of eternal thorns
purpled with the blood, not only of her Lord,
but of all the martyrs who have died in His
name. Too slight has been their use of the
deep and touching pathos, and that voice
" as the sound of many waters" which
sounds in all her liturgy and praises in self-
less giving the " firstborn of all creation,"
Him that was despised and rejected of men.
We are like the heirs of a great house
and park, who have lived only in the kitchen
and never bathed in the lake. All this
may be true, and it is right that we should
regard as coming with authority, *i.e.* as
speaking with a *presumption* in its favour,
the life of devotion, or the round of fast
and festival, or the habits and gestures of
the ministers, or even the tones and hymns
which in the vast experience of ages have
filtered into the Church, making her the
true home of the soul.

And yet we must not forget the other
side. If that view of the nature of a
society we have been setting forth in these

lectures be well founded, and if the claim of the English Church to be a true part of the great universal life be sound, we are not to ignore or treat as of no authority some characteristic qualities of that part. Two dangers there seem to me prevalent just now. The one is that of many who, while repudiating the positive claims of the Papacy, hold yet at bottom to the same theory of the Christian society; *i.e.* they would concentrate its reality in an official caste and leave the society in a position purely passive. That is by no means confined to *soi-disant* Catholics, or even to High Churchmen, and it has been partly increased by the pernicious fact of the parson's freehold. Secondly, there is the danger, perhaps even more widely prevalent, to suppose that anything characteristically English is certainly wrong; and to claim universal or binding authority for some practice or doctrine, which so far from being universal is confined to one portion of the Western Church. Ignorant for the most part of history, and especially of the seventeenth century, and oblivious of the future, such persons would tie men down to an absolute and literal following of what under ultramontane pressure has been forced upon the Churches of Italy, and France, and Spain, and would by implication deny the very claim on which our own corporate existence is based. The notion that it is wrong not to do this or that because it is the custom of Western Christendom can be justified only if the Church of England is no part of it, and leads by logical steps direct to Ultramontanism. That the Church of England has much to learn I would be the last to deny: but is that any ground for supposing that she has nothing to teach? Can anyone who seriously considers the facts believe that to be true of the communion in which, to mention no more, Hooker wrote, and Andrews prayed, and Butler argued, and Liddon preached? I say that it is revolting to talk like this, and it would be absurd were it not so dangerous. Yet many do it. At no time was it more deeply needed to preserve the self-identity and the being not only of the Catholic Church but of "that pure and reformed part of it established in this country." We shall never do this if we think of her as a *pis aller*.

Much that has been said in these lectures will seem commonplace, and some of it obvious. Yet it is plain that the principles here set out are not recognised, and where they are recognised are often disliked. Their purpose will be achieved if I have shown these facts: First, the problem of the relations of Church and State cannot be considered in isolation. It raises topics which go down to the root of all political philosophy, and forces us to face the whole problem of the true nature of civil society and the meaning of personality. If the view which is here suggested be the true one, we must get rid of our enslavement to doctrines never altogether true, but far less true to facts now than has been the case at some periods, as, *e.g.*, in a City-State. We must seek to make our theories grow out of and co-ordinate with the life of men in society as it is lived. We must distrust abstract doctrines of sovereignty, with which the facts can be made to square only by elaborate sophistry. Above all, we must be willing to put liberty above other ends as a political goal, and to learn that true liberty will be found by allowing full play to the uncounted forms of the associative instinct. We are fighting not only our own battle but that of the liberty of all smaller societies against the tendency to mere concentration, which in one way is a marked feature of our time. Much has to be learnt both by ourselves and others from the mediæval guild system. Further, we must learn to allow to others that liberty we claim for ourselves as a corporate society, and fairly face the fact which I have called "the religious heterogeneity of the modern State." Lastly, we shall see that the only basis on which a true defence of the English Church against Rome can be founded is precisely the same as that which we have been expounding. For Rome, as a Church polity, simply embodies those seeming notions of omnipotent sovereignty which we saw had passed over from the antique State to the modern world. And thus we are forced to consider something of the nature of religious authority in general, and of the life of the part in the whole. Perhaps these are enough topics to have suggested in four lectures.

APPENDIX

APPENDIX I

RESPUBLICA CHRISTIANA

I THINK it was Lord Halsbury, in the Scotch Church case, who stopped one of the advocates in his use of the word Church, saying that they as a Court had nothing to do with that, and that they could only consider the question as one concerning a trust. In other words, with a religious society as such they could not deal, but only with a trust or a registered company. This is only one instance of a fact exhibited in the whole of that case: namely, the refusal of the legal mind of our day to consider even the possibility of societies possessing an inherent, self-developing life apart from such definite powers as the State, or the individuals founding the body under State authority, have conferred upon them explicitly. In this view, apart from the State, the real society —and from individuals the living members

of the State — there are no active social
unities ; all other apparent communal unities
are directly or indirectly delegations, either
of State powers or of individuals. To such
a view the notion is abhorrent of a vast
hierarchy of interrelated societies, each alive,
each personal, owing loyalty to the State,
and by it checked or assisted in their action
no less than are private individuals, but no
more deriving their existence from Government concession than does the individual
or the family. In other words, these phrases
of Lord Halsbury are but the natural expression of the concession theory of corporate
life which sees it as a fictitious personality,
created by the State for its own purposes,
and consequently without any natural or
inherent powers of its own. This theory
is not so universally accepted as was once
the case, but Professor Geldart's inaugural
lecture on " Legal Personality " shows how
great are the obstacles still to be encountered
by that theory of realism which is for most
of us associated with the name of Gierke,[1]

[1] Gierke, *Das Deutsche Genossenschaftsrecht*, especially vols. ii. and iii., is the prime authority for the
discussion of this topic in reference alike to historical

and was popularised by Maitland. The latter, moreover, has shown how that very English institution of the *trust* has preserved us from the worse perils of the rigid doctrinaire conception of the civilian. For under the name of a trust many of the qualities of true personality have been able to develop unmolested. But this has not been all to the good. It has probably delayed the victory of the true conception, by enabling us to " muddle through " with the false one. Moreover, the trust is and assimilates itself always rather to the *Anstalt*

development in the ancient mediæval world and in the post-Renaissance State, and to theoretical truth. In another work, *Die Genossenschafts Theorie*, Dr. Gierke shows, by an elaborate analysis of recent decisions both in State and federal courts in Germany, how entirely impossible it is to work with the rigid civilian theory ; and how the courts and judges, while often paying lip-service to " Romanist" notions, are driven in spite of themselves to make use of the more vital Teutonic notions. The whole matter is intimately connected with that conflict described by Beseler in *Das Volksrecht und das Juristenrecht*. There is a short lecture of Gierke, *Das Wesen des Menschlichen Verbandes,* which is also very illuminative. Professor Jethro Brown in an Appendix to the *Austinian Theory of Law and Government* is worthy of study. There is a somewhat meagre account of the various theories in Carr, *The Law of Corporations.*

M

or the *Stiftung* than to the living communal
society, the true corporation, with its basis
in the *Genossenschaft ;* and consequently,
as was proved in this Scotch case, the necessary independence of a self-developing personality is denied to it, and its acts are treated
as invalid on this very ground—that it is only
a trust tied rigidly to its establishing terms,
and not a true society with a living will and
power of change.

However, it is not the truth or falsehood
of the concession theory, or its realist adver-
sary, that I am to discuss here, but rather
its origin. I want to try for a little to see
what lies behind it. The doctrine of which
we speak could hardly be of modern origin.
In the infinitely complex life of modern
civilisation and its religious heterogeneity
we observe, as a matter of actual fact, the
phenomenon of vast numbers of societies
all acting as though they were persons.
They do manage to do all or most of the
things which they would do even if the
concession theory were not dominant. Indeed, it is only by a series of very transparent fictions that their activities are
brought under this rubric. To all intents

and purposes they act, not as fictitious but as real legal personalities. Of course the metaphysical question, what this personality really means, lies outside our limits, just as the question whether the will is free or determined has nothing to do with the State in its treatment of the individual. No one is debarred from believing determinism because the State treats its citizens as free agents. Further than this the *Taff Vale* decision is significant, for it tended to show that corporate life was a thing natural and arising of itself in bodies of men associated for permanent objects, and that it could not be destroyed by the process of ignoring it; in other words, that Trades Unions were personalities, in spite of their own wishes, and in spite of the Act of Parliament which had allowed to them much of the liberty of corporate personality while preserving them from its liabilities. That the House of Lords upheld Mr. Justice Farwell in this case, and at the cost of much odium, is also evidence that the concession theory is not really congruous with the facts of life, and that it is not of modern origin, but is in some way an inheritance from the past. We see, in fact, the horizons of the legal mind changing, and we gather that this mentality must relate to some time when, to speak of the two great bodies whose clash has been unending, State and Church were so bound together in unity that they could not be conceived, either of them, as a separate society with a separate life, but both appeared as different aspects or functionings of one and the same body. Such a time is clearly remote from the world we live in.

Let us now take an instance from a Continental country, France. In France the concession theory has long reigned practically unchecked, alike as a legal theory and even as a political maxim. It burst into renewed activity only the other day in the Associations " Loi." Rousseau and his followers have always been opposed to allowing any inherent rights to bodies other than the sovereign people. There were, at least in earlier theory, rights of man and there were rights of the State. There were no rights of any other society. But for their obsession with this doctrine, the statesmen of the Revolution could never even have dreamt of such a project as the *Constitution Civile* of the clergy.   Now, however, men have gone even further, and deny all rights at all except those of the Republic one and indivisible.   M. Emile Combes put it, writing in an English review, " There are no rights but the rights of the State; there is no authority but the authority of the Republic."   As I said, it is the origin, not the validity, of this conception with which I am concerned this evening.   On this very controversy there was published a volume of collected speeches by M. Combes, with a preface by M. Anatole France.   It is called *Une Campagne Laïque.*   That title contains, in my view, the key to the mystery.   Consider for a moment that M. Combes is not a layman, but an unbeliever; he is a fanatical anti-Christian, and would repudiate with scorn any notion that he was a lay member of the Catholic Church.   He is a Secularist, pure and simple, and the whole campaign for the laicisation of the schools, whether in France, or Spain, or Portugal, is a campaign for their entire secularisation, as we

well know and is never denied. The ludi-
crous difficulties into which the need of
removing all Christian and Theistic reference sometimes leads the compilers of text-
books have been frequently observed.
Laicisation might very well describe the
Kenyon-Slaney clause in England, and is a
not unfair description of some parts of the
undenominationalist movement, for that is,
at least in name, a Christian movement,
and is directed to removing education from
clerical control, direct or indirect, and sub-
stituting a purely lay authority—still
Christian. In France, of course, no such
aim was ever suggested, and the Extremists
have never made any difficulty about
declaring that their object was to *de-
Christianise* the nation. Why, then, should
M. Combes use a term so essentially
ecclesiastical as *lay* to describe his campaign ? I answer that it was because he
could not help it ; the distinction that has
ruled Europe for so many centuries has
been a distinction, not between Christian
and non-Christian societies, but between
cleric and layman, between the spiritual
and the temporal power, each of them

exercised within the Church; between the ecclesiastical and the secular governments, each of them functioning within the body politic. M. Combes used the word *laïque* as an unconscious survival of the day when an attitude similar to his own could have been rightly described by that term. He slipped into it, because the categories of our thought are still ruled by influences that breathe of a different world. He was unconsciously, and in spite of himself, recalling a time when troubles between Church and State were not troubles between two societies, but between two departments of one society; not between Church and State conceived as separate social entities facing one another, like the College and the University, but rather as between Church-men, *i.e.* ecclesiastics, and statesmen, be-tween the King's Court and the Papal *Curia*, between lawyers and bishops, be-tween kings or emperors and popes. Only some sort of odd historical survival affords any explanation of the use of such a term as *laïque* (which has no meaning except in relation to the Church and the clergy) by so violent an anti-Christian as M. Emile

Combes. But this is not all. It seems to point to a narrower use of the term Church than that in vogue to-day. In common parlance the Church in the Middle Ages meant not the *congregatio fidelium*—though, of course, no one would have denied this to be the right meaning—not the whole body of baptized Christians as distinct from those who were not, but rather the active governing section of the Church—the hierarchy and, I suppose, the religious orders. The common use of any term, especially a collective name, is to be found, not by what it sometimes means nor by what it ought to mean by that for which the society stands, but by what other set of people it is used to distinguish from—and this is the case with the word Church. In the Middle Ages the Church is used to distinguish the spirituality from the laity, and in nine cases out of ten it means the ecclesiastical body; in modern times the word Church is used to distinguish Churchmen from Dissenters of one kind or another; so that, whereas in the Middle Ages "I am a Churchman" would mean "I am *not* a layman," nowadays the same phrase means "I am not a Dissenter."[1]

When we talk of the Church we com-

[1] Take the following dialogue from "Twelfth Night" between Viola and the Clown (Act iii. sc. 1):

Vio. Save thee, friend, and thy music. Dost thou live by thy tabor?

Clo. No, sir, I live by the church.

Vio. Art thou a churchman?

Clo. No such matter, sir; I do live by the church; for I do live at my house, and my house doth stand by the church.

Is it not evident here that Churchman means clergyman?

A similar use of the term occurs in the Canons of 1604.

Also in the *Somnium Viridarii* (p. 167) it is definitely stated that there are two jurisdictions:

"Nam in eadem civitate duo sunt populi scilicet clericorum et laicorum, 12 q. 1. c. duo; duo genera simlitum scilicet ecclesiæ et seculi; 1. di. c. clericum qui paganum; pontificalis et regalis potestas, 96 di. cap. duo, et sic duæ jurisdictiones."

I give another instance from the sixteenth century:

"I am more and more in the mind, that it were for the good of the world, that Churchmen did meddle with Ecclesiastick affaires only; that were they never so able otherwise, they are unhappie statesmen; that as Erastiane Cæsaro-Papisme is hurtfull to the Church, so ane Episcopall-Papa-Cæsarisme is unfortunate for the State." (Baillie's *Letters*, iii. 38.)

This is interesting, for it illustrates also the thesis of Lecture III.

monly mean the body of Churchmen as against those who are not Churchmen. The reason is that we live in a society which is religiously heterogeneous; so that no one nowadays thinks of everybody as *ipso facto* in one Church, but as a member of this or that Christian community, all equally tolerated; or, indeed, of many other bodies semi-religious or secular, like the Theistic Church, the Positivist body, the Labour Church, the Theosophists, the Christian Scientists, and so forth.

But even here we are not consistent. In common speech men are always dropping quite unconsciously into the older habit of talk, which treats the Church as primarily the clergy. Let me give an instance common in nearly all our experience. How many a youth has been rebuked by some stiff Churchman, probably an uncle, an archdeacon home from Barbadoes, for saying that he " is going into the Church," when he means taking Holy Orders? He is bidden to remember that he is in the Church as a baptized and confirmed member; that the Church does not mean the clergy; that if that is the sort of doctrine

he is going to preach, he had better adopt
some other calling, &c. &c.

Now I cannot help feeling that the
unfortunate schoolboy has a far better
defence than he commonly imagines. He
might reply in something of this sort:
" True, my dear uncle, I made a slip,
and I regret it. It is less important than
you think. For since you left England for
the Barbadoes, thirty years ago, things have
greatly changed. We live in days of religious chaos, when no one is likely to think
Churchmanship a matter of course. But
I should like to point out to you that if
the phrase I have used is theologically
heretical, which I do not deny, it is *his-
torically orthodox*, and by my use of it (a
pure slip, due to the uprush of the sub-
liminal consciousness) I am witnessing to
the unity of history in a way which, with
all your correct Tractarianism, you fail to
comprehend. In the Middle Ages, and
indeed a very long time since the Middle
Ages, as you may see if you will study
novels, the Church did mean in ordinary
speech the Church as an effectively organised
body, a hierarchy (there were no Houses of

Laymen in those days), and nonconformity to the established religion was either non-existent or a crime. If you and I had been living in the thirteenth, fourteenth, or even the sixteenth century, and I had ventured to say to a person of your dignity (for your dignity was as great as your chances of salvation were said to be small in those days), 'I belong to the Church,' meaning by it I belong to that branch of the Church established in this realm, what would have happened? You would have been surprised, nay shocked. You would have charged me with incipient heresy because to say I am a Churchman in that sense implies that I have my choice, and that, if I chose, I might be something else. Even to contemplate such a possibility borders upon heresy. If not treason, it is very near akin to *misprision of treason* to Holy Church. And as your nephew I should have been fortunate to have escaped with a sound avuncular whipping. If, however, I had said I belong to the Church, meaning by it what you have just rebuked me for—meaning, namely, I am a clerk in Holy Orders, or in minor orders going on to greater things—then you would have quite understood me. You would have strongly approved, and you would doubtless have given me, though only sixteen and a half years old, a couple of livings and one prebend to be held in plurality, and *in commendam* with a *non-obstante* dispensation from the Holy Father permitting absence, in view of the other livings and offices which a person so important as an archdeacon's nephew would certainly have held. So I'll trouble you, after all, for that five-pound note you threatened to withdraw."

That is the point. The word Churchman means to-day one who belongs to the Church as against others. In the Middle Ages there were no others, or, if there were, they were occupied in being burnt. A Churchman meant one who belonged to the Church in the narrower sense of its governing body—an ecclesiastic, as the word implies ; just as statesman to-day means not a member but an officer, actual or potential, of the State. In mediæval Europe folk would be more doubtful whether you were an Englishman or Bavarian than whether you were or were not a Churchman in our sense, but they might be greatly concerned to know whether you were clerk or layman. Churchmanship was co-extensive with citizenship, and, indeed, with more than citizenship, but the Church as a hierarchy was not; it was not the realm, but an estate of the realm.

When the Church came in conflict, as it often did, with the State, it meant the clash of the ecclesiastical with the civil hierarchy of officials. Both these bodies were composed of Churchmen, in our sense, and existed in one society—the commonwealth.

All this leads to the main thesis of this paper—that in the Middle Ages Church and State in the sense of two competing societies did not exist; you have instead the two official hierarchies, the two departments if you will: the Court and the *Curia*, the kings' officials and the popes'. But in these controversies you have practically no conception of the Church, as consisting of the whole body of the baptized set over against the State, consisting of the same people, only viewed from a different standpoint and organised for a different end. It is a quarrel between two different sets of people—the lay officials and the clerical, the bishops and the justices, the pope and the kings; it is not thought of under that highly complex difficult form of a quarrel between two societies, each of which was composed of precisely the same persons, only one is called the State, for it deals with temporal ends, and the other Church, as the Christian community. Such a notion would be possible only if the sense of corporate personality in Church and State had been fully developed. This was not the case. The conception of the State was indeed very inchoate, and there was very little power of distinguishing it from its officials; and even in the Church this weakness led to the increasing power of the popes, for the Church took over its conceptions of government from the ancient world, and the Republic had latterly been entirely identified with the emperors.[1] There was no personal sub-

[1] *Cf.* the notion of the Church when "von der Kirche als Rechtssubjekt die Rede sei. Dies sei die Bedeutung von Ecclesia im Sinne des lokalen Verbandes. *Einen solchen aber konnte man bei der damaligen Verfassung naturgemäss nicht in der Gemeinde, sondern lediglich in der klerikalen Genossenschaft finden.* Und so kam man zu einer Definition, wie sie Placentinus

stratum behind of which he was the mere representative.

To make my meaning clear let me quote two passages from Maitland's *Lectures on*

aufstellt: *ecclesia dicitur collectio constituorum vel coadunatio virorum vel mulierum in aliquo sacro loco constitutarum ad serviendum Deo.* So war in der That die Kirche als Rechtssubjekt in das korporativ Schema gebracht und man konnte ohne Weiteres die *Ecclesia* zu den *Universitates* und *Collegia* rechnen und den für diese geltenden Rechtssätzen unterstellen. Ja es sollte ihr, weil sie die privilegiirteste unter den Korporationen sei, kein bei irgend einer Korporation vorkommendes Recht fehlen können, weshalb sie namentlich der *respublica* und *civitas* gleichgestellt wurde." (Gierke, iii. 195–6.)

Again he cites the following in the notes: "Si enim aliqua universitas privilegiata est, hodie, potius privilegiata est ecclesia." " Ecclesia aequiparatur reipublicae." But this is of individual churches. "Weniger als je wurde den Gemeinden irgend ein aktives kirchliches Recht verstattet, immer entschiedener trat die Kirche, als ein fremder und äusserer Körper dem Volk gegenüber. Erschien sie dem Deutschen dieser Zeit vorzugsweise als eine grosse Innung oder Zunft, so war sie ihm doch keineswegs eine Innung aller Gläubigen, eine Gemeinschaft, die jeder Laie mit einem Teil seiner Persönlichkeit bilden half, sondern sie war ihm die Zunft des geistlichen Standes. . . . Freilich war es dem Laien unerlässlich für sein Seelenheil, an dem von der Kirche besessenen und verwalteten Heilsschatz Anteil zu erlangen; aber zu diesem Behuf verhandelte und verkehrte er mit ihr

Constitutional History. On pp. 101–2 we read :
" While we are speaking of this matter of sovereignty, it will be well to remember

wie mit einer dritten Person, kaum anders wie mit der Kaufmanns oder Gewerbezunft, wenn er ihrer Waaren bedurfte. *Die Kirche war in Allem ein geistlicher Staat für sich,* in welchem der Laie keines Bürgerrechts genoss." (Gierke, i. 427 ; *cf.* also ₁287.) " Bei dieser Auffassung der staatlichen Rechtssubjectivität konnten es die Römer zu Wort und Begriff der Staatspersönlichkeit nicht bringen. Sie blieben bei der Subjectivität des *populus,* und später des Kaisers stehen. Diese Subjectivität aber unterstellten sie, weil einzig in ihrer Art, keinem höheren Gattungsbegriff." (Gierke, iii. 50, *Das Deutsche Genossenschaftsrecht.*) *Cf.* also the following passage in regard to the Church. After describing the Church as God-planted, " Wenn einer so konstruirten Gesammtkirche Rechtspersönlichkeit beigelegt wird, so kann Quelle derselben nicht *die den Körper bildende Gesammtheit, sondern lediglich Gott und mittelbar dessen irdischer Stellvertreter sein.* In der That hat daher nach der Lehre der Kanonisten der göttliche Stifter selbst seiner Kirche zugleich mit der Heilsvollmacht die für deren Durchführung erforderliche Rechtssubjektivität verliehen. Und allein von Gott und seinem Vikar sind fort und fort alle einzelnen Privilegien und Rechte abzuleiten, welche der Gesammtkirche um ihres geistlichen Berufes willen zustehen, während auch die höchste weltliche Macht diese Rechte nicht zu mindern, sondern nur rein weltliche Privilegien hinzuzufügen vermag. Ebenso aber findet

N

that our modern theories run counter to the deepest convictions of the Middle Ages— to their whole manner of regarding the relation between Church and State. *Though they may consist of the same units, though every man may have his place in both organisms, these two bodies are distinct. The State has its king or emperor, its laws, its legislative assemblies, its courts, its judges; the Church has its pope, its prelates, its councils, its laws, its courts.* That the Church is in any sense below the State no one will maintain, that the State is below the Church is a more plausible doctrine; but the general conviction is that the two are independent, that neither derives its authority from the other. Obviously, when men think thus, while they more or less consistently act upon this theory, they have no sovereign in Austin's sense; before

die einheitliche Kirchenpersönlichkeit ihren obersten Träger und Repraesentanten nicht in der Gesammtheit, sondern in Gott selbst und mittelbar in dessen irdischem Statthalter, so dass sogar als Subjekt der Rechte, welche für die *ecclesia universalis* in Anspruch genommen werden, Gott oder Christus selbst und vertretungsweise dann auch der Papst bezeichnet werden kann." (Gierke, iii. 249, 250.)

the Reformation Austin's doctrine was impossible."

In regard to the theory of sovereignty, this statement is doubtless true of the smaller States. It is not true of the Papacy; the *plenitudo potestatis* being simply sovereignty in the Austinian sense, developed by the canonists from Roman law and applied to the Pope. It is not true of the more extreme Imperialist doctrine; the lawyers who told Frederic Barbarossa that the property of all his subjects was really his, were, in theory at least, strong Austinians, as was the normal civilian. Indeed, it is from Rome, first imperial then papal, *i.e.* from civil and canon law, that the modern doctrine of sovereignty derives. In its modern form it goes through the mediæval canonists to Renaissance thinkers like Bodin, thence through Hobbes and the supporters of Divine Right to Austin. Even in the fourteenth century it is applied to the minor States. Baldus, I believe, was the first to say that *rex est imperator in regno suo*, and we find one of our own kings claiming to be *entier empereur dans son royaume*, and this, the claim to sovereignty, is the true meaning of the preamble to the great statute of appeals, " this realm of England is an Empire." Moreover, it is not quite true to assert that no one said that the Church ought to be below the State. For that is the exact argument of the twelfth-century Erastian treatise by Gerard of York, printed by Böhmer in the *Libelli de Lite.* He declares, indeed, not that the Church is below the State, but that, in the one commonwealth, which you can call either kingdom or church at your pleasure, the secular power is above the ecclesiastical. Still, of course, it is true that in the main Austinian doctrine is not applicable to the feudal commonwealth of the Middle Ages.

It is not of this matter that I want to speak at length, but of the sentences in italic. Later on in the book there is an even more emphatic expression of the same view:

" The mediæval theory of the relation between Church and State seems this, that they are independent organisms consisting nevertheless of the same units " (p. 506).

To that statement I say *quod non.* I

make this criticism with much diffidence, for every word that Maitland wrote is worth its weight in gold. Yet we must remember that these lectures were not written to be published, and that they were delivered in 1887, before he entered upon those studies which resulted in his work on *The Canon Law* and his translation of Gierke. To say the very least, it is not certain that he would have written thus fifteen years later. Nor, again, do I desire to assert an " absolute not." I do not deny that such a view of Church and State was possible to acute minds in the Middle Ages, any more than I assert that because men normally meant by the Church the hierarchy they did not frequently mean the *congregatio fidelium*. I think that in the later Middle Ages men were moving in that direction. Judging by his letters and manifestoes, I think it not impossible that Frederic II held this view or something like it. What I do think is that this view in no way repre- sented the ruling thought of the Middle Ages, that it was not the necessary back- ground of their minds, that all, or nearly all, the evidence points the other way, and that, if we accepted Maitland's view, we should be left with no intelligible explanation of certain phenomena in the sixteenth century, to say nothing of existing controversies and modes of thought.

When we do find one pope speaking of God's vicar as master both of the terrene and the spiritual empire, he shows by his words that he cannot think of them apart. The notion of a single society is so universal that, even where in words the popes admit two, it is in order to deny it in fact and to claim for themselves the lordship of both.[1]

Moreover, when the Inquisition handed a heretic over to the secular arm, what was intended by the figure? Surely, that the

---

[1] Quæ nimirum inter cetera dulcedinis suæ verba illud nobis videbantur consulere, per quod et status imperii gloriosius regitur et sanctæ ecclesiæ vigor solidatur; videlicet ut sacerdotium et imperium in unitate concordiæ coniugantur. Nam sicut duabus oculis humanum corpus temporali lumine regitur, ita his duabus dignitatibus in pura religione concordantibus corpus ecclesiæ spirituali lumine regi et illuminari probatur. (Gregor VII to Rudolf of Suabia, Jaffé, *Regis.*, i. 19.)

This is a fair sample of the usual way of regarding it. Later on in the *Somnium Viridarii* it is denied that two jurisdictions imply two States.

two arms, the secular and spiritual powers, were arms of the same body—or else the metaphor makes nonsense. Yet the view we combat would make two different bodies.

Let me put before you the following considerations : Is it not rather improbable that this difficult position of two corporate bodies, each of the same individual persons though totally distinct as corporate personalities, should have been thought of in a world whose ideals were symbolised in the Holy Roman Empire, whose true respublica is the *civitas Dei*? Even in our own day, when there is so much to favour it, views of this sort, at least in regard to established Churches, are not accepted readily or without argument. How would it have been possible in a world where the unbaptized and the excommunicate were outlaws, and citizenship and Christianity were inextricably bound up? Nobody in the Middle Ages denied that the king was God's minister, or that the bishops were great lords in the commonwealth. Pope and emperor, when they quarrelled, quarrelled like brothers, as members of the same society, the *civitas Dei*.

The fact is, *ecclesia* and *respublica* are more often than not convertible terms in mediæval literature. One writer, who is well known, describes (much in Maitland's way) "a system of two sets of law and courts"; but it is of two sets of people that he is thinking—the clergy and the laity, and it is within the whole—the one society, the *civitas*, which he says is the *ecclesia*— that these two bodies are to be found. I do not say but that later on, after the crystallisation of national States and the development through St. Thomas of the habit of arguing about the Church as one among a class of political societies, some such view as Maitland suggests may not have been now and then discernible. But I think it was very rare.

And what we want to know is not how some theorist formulated the matter, but what were the "common thoughts of our forefathers." Supposing that I had gradu- ated, not at Cambridge but at Bologna in the thirteenth century, that I was a *doctor in utroque jure*, a protonotary apostolic and au auditor of the rota, should I have declared the kingdom or the empire to be a society quite distinct from the Church, though containing the same units? I trow not. I am much more likely to have said that the limits of the kingly power were determined by the Church, meaning the hierarchy, and that the king must do his duty because he was the minister of God and must therefore be subject to His vicar. So far from denying the king *qua* king to be a member of the same society as my own, I should have made his membership the ground of a due reverence for *protonotaries apostolic.* Supposing, again, I had been a clerk of the king's court or a royal justice or one of the barons at Merton, who were not going to have the laws of England changed to suit the bishops, should I have asserted that they were members of a different State; should I not rather have claimed that, though specially and even reprehensibly privileged, though forming a distinct order in the commonwealth, they were yet English lieges and should be made, willy-nilly, to do and forbear those things lawful to English lieges, and none others? Even if— pardon the impertinence—I had been either a pope on the one hand or an emperor on the other, should I have thought of my rival as the head of another society with which my own relations were strictly international? Hardly. I should rather have deemed him a "dear colleague," and felt it as a God-imposed duty to prevent him injuring his character by attempting a dictation over me, which for God's cause and solely as a matter of duty I was determined to resist. Nor was there warrant in antiquity for this notion of the two societies. The conception of a religious society as distinct from the State had not dawned upon the unified civilisation of Greece and Rome. It was alien alike from the City-State and the Pagan Empire. When it did dawn upon some men's minds, what was the universal response? *Christiani ad leones.* Sir William Ramsay has made it clear that the persecution of the early Church was a matter of policy, and that it was directed against this very notion, the claim to be a separate society, while still remaining Roman citizens. It was the Church as upholding "a new non-Roman unity" that men feared. The primitive Church was without question a society

distinct from the Roman State.[1] As she grew
to strength, and threatened to absorb the
whole population, there was every likelihood
of the view arising which was outlined by
Maitland. But it did not arise. The old conception,
that of Pagan and Jew, was too strong for
it. After Constantine granted the peace of

[1] "Dagegen lag allerdings von vornherein eine
gewaltige negative Umwälzung der antiken Anschau-
ungen von Staat und Recht in *den vom Wesen des
Christenthums untrennbaren Principien* welche dem staatlichen Verbande einen grossen Theil seines bisherigen
Inhalts zu Gunsten der religiösen Gemeinschaft und
des Individuums entzogen. Einmüthig bekannte man
sich zu dem Glauben, dass das innere Leben der
Einzelnen und ihrer religiös-sittlichen Verbände keiner
weltlichen Macht unterworfen und über die Sphäre
der staatlichen Daseinsordnung erhaben sei. *Damit
entschwand die allumfassende Bedeutung des Staats.* Der
Mensch gieng nicht mehr im Bürger, die Gesellschaft
nicht mehr im Staate auf. Das grosse Wort, dass man
Gott mehr gehorchen soll als den Menschen, begann
seinen Siegeslauf. Vor ihm versank die Omnipotenz
des heidnischen Staats. Die Idee der immanenten
Schranken aller Staatsgewalt und aller Unterthanen-
pflicht leuchtete auf. Das Recht und die Pflicht des
Ungehorsams gegen staatlichen Gewissenszwang
wurden verkündigt und mit dem Blute der Märtyrer
besiegelt." (Gierke, *op. cit.*, iii. 123.) *Cf.* also the
author's remarks on the effect of St. Augustine's *De
Civitate Dei.* (*Ibid.*, 124–7.)

the Church, it was not long, at most three-quarters of a century, before the old conception ruled again of a great unity in which civil and ecclesiastical powers were merely separate departments. Had the world been ripe for toleration of rival bodies things might have been very different. But it was not ripe. The emperors, as you know, were treated almost as ecclesiastical powers; coercion was employed on both sides in the Arian controversy; finally the Catholics conquered under Theodosius the Great. Arianism was made a crime; Paganism was suppressed; and the world was ripe for that confusion of baptism and citizenship which ruled the Middle Ages. True, there were many struggles between the different authorities, and their issues varied with time and place. But neither emperors nor prelates were treated as rulers of rival societies. The *Code of Justinian* was compiled subsequently to the *De Civitate Dei* of St. Augustine. The whole spirit of both tends to identify Church and State, although neither quite realised this.[1] The Pagan

---

[1] See on the Byzantine view of the two powers, Mr. Lacey's remarks in *Marriage in Church and State*.

State was also a Church, and the mediæval Church was also a State; *the* Church and *the* State in theory. Each governs the whole of life, and the problem is not whether you take power from one society and give it to the other, but where you tilt the balance of authority—on to the side of the lay officials or to that of the clerics. Shall power belong to him who wields the sword or to him who instructs the wielder? Roman Law, as it entered the mediæval world, is the law of a mediævalised empire, and the code begins with the rubric, *De Summa Trinitate et Fide Catholica.* Much of the liberty afterwards claimed by canonists could be supported by adroit quotations from the imperial law.

All this was crystallised in the idea of the *Holy Roman Empire*, the governing conception of a great Church-State, of which it is hard to say whether it is a religious or a temporal institution. Half the trouble came from the fact that popes and emperors were heads, in theory co-equal, of the same society. The argument so constantly repeated, that the unity of the society needs a single person as the centre, and that, therefore, the secular power must be subject to the spiritual, owes its force to the very fact that men were incapable of seeing two societies, and that the theory of two co-equal heads under Christ as King did not work in practice. The pope, we must remember, is the emperor's archbishop; foreign he might be to England and France as nationality crystallised, but no emperor could afford to treat him as foreign. That would have been to give up all claims to Italy.

The lesser conflicts were all conducted under the shadow of this conception. Although in countries like England or France it may have been easier to see the distinctions of the two powers, its meaning was not grasped till later, and men did not talk of two societies, separate though composed of the same individuals.

But it will be said, what of the Canon Law? Here is a separate body of legal rules modelled in its form on the civil law and claiming sometimes to override it, possessed of a higher sanction, so that towards the close of the Middle Ages a French writer can say that *omnia jura civilia sunt canonica.*[1]

Now it is true that in so far as the Canon Law governed the laity, and existed by the side of national laws, its existence points towards a belief in two distinct social organisms; yet I do not think that this inference was drawn at the time. The passage I alluded to above treats it as mainly *law for the clergy*, and so far as that was usual, this view would tally with all I have

[1] The following passages are a fair indication of the common view : "Si auctoritas sacra pontificum et potestas imperialis vere glutino caritatis adinvicem complerentur; nihil est enim in præsenti seculo pontifice clarius, nihil rege sublimius." *Cf.* also Henry IV to Greg. VII (Jaffé, *Bib. Rer. Ger.,* ii. 46) : "Cum enim regnum et sacerdotium, ut in Christo rite administrata subsistant, vicaria sua ope semper indigeant." From the following sentence from the Deposition of Frederic II, it can readily be seen how intimately connected are canon and civil law : "Nonne igitur hec non levia, sed efficacia sunt argumenta de suspicione heresis contra eum, cum tamen hereticorum vocabulo *illos jus civile contineri asserat,* et latis adversus eos sentenciis debere subcumbere qui vel levi argumento a judicio catholice religionis et tramite detecti fuerint deviare ?" (Deposition of Frederic II. Huillard-Bréholles, *Historia Diplomatica F. II,* vi. 326.) Elsewhere he is accused of treason towards the pope : "Non sine proditionis nota, et lese crimine majestatis." (*Ibid.,* 322.)

been saying. The popes, however, doubtless thought they were legislating for all Christians, but these popes were claiming a *plenitudo potestatis* over kings and princes, which implied that all secular law was merely allowed by them. Moreover, in those days of feudal courts, men were in the habit of seeing every kind of competing jurisdiction without definitely claiming that it destroyed such unity in the State as they were accustomed to see. The very looseness of structure of the mediæval State, if we are to use the term, enabled the canonists to do their work alongside of the secular courts without drawing all the conclusions we should do. Unification was the work of the Renaissance and the Reform, and it was not till then that men would come to argue that it must either exist by the allowance, express or tacit, of the prince, or else that the prince must be in reality a subject.

Moreover, I do not think people sufficiently realise how systems, apparently competing, went on together in practice. Legal writers, like Bartolus on the one hand or Innocent IV on the other, quote the canon law and the civil law indiscriminately, and never seem conscious of them as being the laws of two separate societies. I cannot find this conception in Innocent's great commentary on the *Decretale* of Gregory IX. Bartolus wrote a treatise on the differences between the two systems, but there is no hint that he regarded them as the laws of two different States.[1] The fact is that it was the two together, treated as an ideal rather than coercive law, which ruled men's minds; and out of this amalgam rose modern politics and international law.

Again, if you take the *Unam Sanctam* of Boniface VIII, that does not assert the power of the Church over the State. Rather it asserts the power of the Pope over every human being.[2] In fact the personalisation

[1] It is not certain that this attribution is correct. But it makes no difference to this point whether the book was by Bartolus or another lawyer.

[2] *Cf.* Henry of Cremona's interesting treatise on behalf of Boniface VIII, printed in Scholz, *Die Publizistik zur Zeit Philipps des Schönen,* App. 475. The heavenly hierarchy has its ranks and orders, so also has the earthly :—

Nam sunt diversi ordines et diverse potestates ecclesiastice et seculares et ultima est summus pon-

of authority in popes, kings, and feudal lords and prelates was one of the causes that retarded the growth of such theory as that of the two kinds of *societas perfecta*. The conflicts between the two powers are habitually spoken of as struggles between the *sacerdotium* and the *regnum*; although the wider terms *respublica* and *ecclesia* are not unknown, it is surely reasonable to interpret them by the former. I give one or two stanzas of a doggerel poem by Gualterus de Insula from the *Libelli de Lite*.[1] They represent the natural categories into which men's thoughts fell when they discussed the topic.

tifex, in quo omnes potestates agregantur, et ad quem reducuntur et ad quem tamquam in simplicissinum terminantur et ad quod designandum summus pontifex in coronacione sua mitram seu coronam portat in capite, que a base seu inferiori parte lata incipit et terminatur in simplici cornu, quia latitudo et diversitas omnium ordinum et potestatum in persona ipsius summi pontificis terminantur et ad eum reducuntur.

Is it possible that a passage like this would have been written in a day when Church and State were conceived as two societies, each consisting of the same units?

---

[1] iii. 559–60.

" Per Noe colligimus summum patriarcham
Totius ecclesiae caput et monarcham.

Ergo vel ecclesiae membrum non dicatur
Cæsar, vel pontifici summo supponatur.

Major et antiquior est imperialis
Dignitas quam cleri sit vel pontificalis,
' Major ' dico tempore, semper enim malis
Regibus subiacuit terra laycalis.

Imperator Esau major quidem natu,
Papa quidem Jacob est, minor enim statu :
Ille sceptro rutilat, iste potentatu,
Ille major viribus, iste dominatu.

Cæsar habet gladium sed materialem,
Hunc eundem pontifex sed spiritualem.
Cæsar ergo suscipit usum temporalem
Ab eo, qui possidet curam pastoralem.

Igitur si vera sunt ista quae promisi
Nichil habet penitus imperator, nisi
Ab eo, qui possidet claves paradisi,
At Petri vicarius : *non est sua phisi.*"

The famous passage of Pope Gelasius about
the two powers, so often quoted, is no evidence the other way ; it refers to the two
governing authorities of the *mundus*, which
one writer declares to mean the State, not

two separate societies. Its date alone is sufficient proof that it had reference to the Christianised ancient empire, when such a division was not to be thought of.

John of Salisbury, in his *Policraticus*, holds very high views of the function of the priest in the State, but it is a power within, not outside, the State that is to rule it, like the soul in the body.

One writer, Jordan of Osnabruck, equates the three powers, the *sacerdotium*, the *imperium*, and the *studium*, as all equally needful for the health of the Church. The *sacerdotium* he assigns to the Romans as the senior, the *imperium* to the Germans, and the *studium* to the French as being more perspicacious. That such a view could even be thought of is evidence how far asunder were the mediæval notions on the subject from those natural to us.[1]

---

[1] *Cf.* Jordanus von Osnabruck, *Buch über das Römische Reich* (ed. Waitz, p. 71).

Debitus et necessarius ordo requirebat, ut sicut Romani tamquam seniores sacerdotio, sic Germani vel Franci tamquam juniores imperio, et ita Franci quæ vel Gallici tamquam perspicatiores scientiarum studio dotarentur, et ut fidem catholicam quam Romanorum constantia firmiter tenet, illam Germanorum magnani-

Wyclif, in his *Speculum Militantis Ecclesiae*, declares that the ecclesia or commonwealth consists of three sections—lords, clergy, and commons. The argument of the book is that if the Church were disendowed the nobles would be richer and have less motive to oppress the poor. Whether that result followed the dissolution of the monasteries we need not here determine. What is certain is that it never occurred to him to conceive of Church and State as two distinct societies composed of the same units. The same is the case with Marsilius; but

mitas imperialiter tenere precipiat, et eandem Gallicorum argutia et facundia ab omnibus esse tenendam firmissimis rationibus approbet et demonstret. Hiis siquidem tribus, scilicet sacerdotio imperio et studio, tamquam tribus virtutibus, videlicet vitali, naturali et animali, sancta ecclesia katholica spiritualiter, vivificatur, augmentatur et regitur. Hiis etiam tribus, tamquam fundamento pariete et tecto, eadem ecclesia quasi materialiter perficitur. Et notandum quod, sicut ecclesie materiali unum fundamentum et unum tectum sufficit, sed unus paries non sufficit, sic sacerdotio una sedes principalis, videlicet Roma et studio unus locus principalis, videlicet Parisiis sufficit: sed imperio quatuor loca principalia sancti Spiritus ordinatione novimus attributa, que sunt Aquisgrani, Arelatum Mediolanum et urbis Roma.

his Erastianism is so marked that it may
be thought that his evidence is not to the
point. It is notable, however, that he
states (while disapproving the fact) that in
ordinary use the Church meant the clergy
and not the whole Christian people; at
least, he says, that is the most common
usage.

Lastly, let us note the surprise of Archbishop Whitgift at the doctrine of two
societies. Cartwright, the Presbyterian
protagonist, was strongly imbued with the
notion of two kingdoms. Whitgift seems
hardly able to believe his eyes as he reads
it. This comes out *passim* in Whitgift's
answer to Cartwright.

I need hardly point out that this is also
the view of Hooker. And that is the point.
How did that view arise? The very general
Erastianism of most of the Reformers is
well known. It came from this very fact.
Society being conceived as fundamentally
one, and the clergy in their eyes not having
done their part in removing abuses, recourse
must be had to the other power in the
Church, the secular government. When
Luther appealed to the German princes to

take up the work of Reform he did not
mean that he was appealing from the Christian Church to a secular State, but merely
from the clerical to the civil authority.
Any other view is preposterous.

My point is that this distinction of the
two societies is either very primitive, dating
from the days of persecution, or else very
modern, dating from the religious divisions
of Europe. I think that it came about in
some such way as this:

(1) The analysis of political forms, begun
by St. Thomas on the Aristotelian basis, set
on foot the habit of reasoning about political
societies. The facts of the great schism and
the Conciliar movement drove men to discuss
the character and constitution of the Church,
considered as a community, and comparable
to States and kingdoms.

(2) This tendency was furthered by the
growth of national States, by the decay of
feudalism, and by the practical abeyance
of the Holy Roman Empire; although,
even after Constance, the concordats are
not between Church and State, but between
pope and king, bishops and nobles, &c., of
France or other countries.

(3) Then came the Reformation. So far as this was political and princely it made no difference, save that it tilted the balance of power from the clerical to the lay officials. On the other hand in the Empire, as a whole, religious unity was destroyed, and after the Religious Peace of Augsburg the Church could no longer be identified with the Empire. But where either prince or people were not able to make their own religion supreme or universal within the territorial State, the conception of two distinct societies tended to grow up. It is not really in the thought of Calvin, but the organisation of the Huguenots was very important in influencing men's minds. It was so local, so compact, so distinct, that it helped to forward the idea among all persons placed as they were. I do not think that Knox, any more than the other reformers, had any real notion of this distinction. But towards the end of Elizabeth's reign it is certainly to be found in Cartwright and the whole English Presbyterian movement. Andrew Melville developed it in Scotland; and Robert Browne, the originator of the Independents, was inspired by

this notion in the pamphlet *Reformation Without Tarrying for Any.*

In England both the Laudian and the Puritan party were mediævalist ; they believed in a State which was also a Church, and were essentially theocratic. However, the theory of the distinctness of the two societies was beginning to be asserted. It is the burden of Thorndike's *Discourse on the Right of the Church in a Christian State,* and Stillingfleet in his *Irenicum* definitely developed the doctrine in the appendix on Excommunication. The perception was probably due to the outburst of extreme Erastianism in the Long Parliament. What chiefly developed the contrary notion was the non-juring schism. This compelled its adherents, and many High Churchmen who were not its adherents, to think of the Church as the body of all the faithful with rights and powers inherent and unconnected with the State. Union with Scotland increased this tendency, for there was thus before men's eyes the spectacle of two different established Churches. Thus Hoadly gives no hint of any other notion than the old, and his idea of toleration was merely a comprehensive Erastianism, very similar to certain schemes we hear of now. Warburton, on the other hand, develops explicitly and in set terms, in his *Alliance between Church and State*, the doctrine that the two are independent organisms consisting of the same individuals, but existing for different ends, each to be treated as a *corporate personality*. His theory comes at the end, not at the beginning of the development I have been describing, and I cannot help feeling it would have been incomprehensible to men such as Gerard of York or St. Thomas of Canterbury. I should also add that the Jesuits, who had to consider the question of the relations of Church and State in reference to the changed conditions of a divided Europe, were forward in developing the notion of the two societies. In Gierke's view they were the first to develop a frankly secular theory of the State. On the other hand, royalists like Barclay in France, who were yet strong Catholics, in order to combat Bellarmine's doctrine of the indirect temporal sovereignty of the Pope, were driven to be equally explicit as to the State being a *societas perfecta* no less than the

Church, and to claim that the two societies were in a sense distinct.

But it may be asked, What difference does all this make? Nobody denies that Henry IV went to Canossa,[1] or that Boniface VIII issued the *Unam Sanctam*, or that Frederic Barbarossa held the papal stirrup, or that his grandson was deposed by a Church council. What difference can it possibly make whether we assert that these incidents were the result of conflicts between two separate societies, each of them a State, or between two sets of officials in one and the same society? If what has been said is well founded, we must view these conflicts as of the nature of civil war. Does that get us any "forrarder"? If I were a scientific historian I should use great and desolate words about truth, and say that the less it mattered the better was it worth studying. However, instead of this I shall make the modest claim that such view helps us to understand better both history and ourselves.

(1) It explains the quick drop into Eras-

[1] At least I do not. I understand that doubt has been thrown even on this event.

tianism all over Europe in the sixteenth century. The campaign of the Reformers was just *une campagne laïque.* They were not attempting to take power out of the Christian society, but merely out of its clerical officials. All coercive power was to be rested in the prince, but in theory it was always the godly prince, "most religious." So long as they had him on their side, men so different as Laud and Luther felt that they were safe. The sixteenth century witnessed an undoubted victory of the secular over the ecclesiastical power; but it was not for the secular power as a society distinct from the Church, it was a victory for the temporal authority within the one society which can be called either Church or State according to the aspect prominent at the moment. Erastus himself declared that he was only discussing the case of a State which tolerated but a single religion *eamque veram,* a statement which shows how far he is removed from the modern form of the system, which derives its name from him.

(2) Many problems and controversies of modern times are rendered more intelligible

to us, if we adopt the view which I suggest.
Slowly, but only very slowly, has the notion
of separate societies with inherent rights
developed, just as it is only now that the
doctrine of true corporate personality is
being realised. The *Kultur-kampf* was
simply due to the incapacity of Bismarck
to realise that there could be any corporate
life with inherent powers of its own, un-
willing to accept the *sic volo, sic jubeo* of
the State. As we saw, the same notion
was at bottom of the difficulties in the
Free Church of Scotland Appeals. Nor
does it take much ingenuity to discover it
lurking in recent judicial pronouncements
about the *Deceased Wife's Sister Act*, or
about the controversy between Churches
and undenominationalism in regard to
education.[1]

[1] " Hinsichtlich der Enstehung der Korporation geht
das Corpus Juris durchweg von der Auffassung aus,
dass aus der natürlichen oder gewollten Vereinigung von Individuen zwar das thatsächliche Substrat,
niemals jedoch die rechtliche Existenz einer Verbandseinheit hervorzugehen vermag. Vielmehr stammt
zunächst die publicistische Verbandswesenheit während
der Staat selbst als die mit und über den Individuen
gegebene Allegemeinheit keiner Zurückführung auf

(3) The unity of history is a cant phrase and is often made to bear a burden too heavy. But it may be pointed out how strong a testimony to this doctrine is afforded by the persistent notion of the republic, one and indivisible, which has come down to the modern world by descent through the mediæval papacy, the Christian-

einen besonderen rechtlichen Begründungsakt bedarf, auf allen übrigen Stufen vom Staat. *Staatliche Verleihung gilt als die Quelle der publicistischen Existenz auch solcher Gemeinwesen,* welche vor ihrem Eintritt in das römische *jus publicum* als selbständige Staaten bestanden haben; aus staatlicher Verleihung fliesst die Korporationsqualität auch derjenigen Verbände, deren thatsächliches Dasein freier Vereinigung verdankt wird; auf staatliche Verleihung gründet sich die publicistische Verbandseinheit auch der christlichen Kirche, welche selbst ihren Bestand aus göttlicher Stiftung herleitet. Ueberall aber verfährt hierbei der Staat hinsichtlich des rechtlichen Elementes der engeren Verbandswesenheiten wahrhaft konstitutiv. *Alle körperschaftliche Existenz erscheint als das Werk frei schaffender Gesetzgebung,* durch welche der Staat, sei es in der Form der *lex specialis* für das einzelne Gebilde, oder sei es in der Form genereller Regeln für einen Komplex gleichartiger Verbände, seine eigne Gliederung setzt und ordnet. Darum bedarf es auch in keiner Weise einer Normirung bestimmter Voraussetzungen für die Errichtung einer Korporation." (Gierke, *op. cit.,* iii. 142–3.)

ised ancient empire, and the pagan empire, whither it migrated from the compact all-absorbing City-State. Mr. Carlyle, in the first chapter of his history of political theory in the West, was able to show us how the doctrines of Rousseau anent the fundamental equality of man and modern democracy can be found implicit in the Roman jurists, in Cicero, and to witness to a change in feeling between the aristocratic doctrine of Aristotle and the universalist theories of the great republic. This view has been encountered in our own day by the revival of aristocracy proclaimed by Nietzsche, and the doctrines of the fundamental inequality of men based partly on the subjugation of the tropics, partly on Darwinian theories of natural selection and the struggle for existence. The doctrine, however, which I have been considering is even more venerable than that of human equality. For it goes back, with hardly a break, to the omnicompetent and universally penetrating supervision of Sparta and Athens. It is only when we have traced it right back to its origin that we see its inapplicability to the complex life of a modern world-empire.

The theory of sovereignty, whether proclaimed by John Austin or Justinian, or shouted in conflict by Pope Innocent or Thomas Hobbes, is in reality no more than a venerable superstition. It is true to the facts only in a cosy, small and compact State, although by a certain amount of strained language and the use of the maxim, " whatever the sovereign permits he commands," it can be made not logically untenable for any conditions of stable civilisation. As a fact it is as a series of groups that our social life presents itself, all having some of the qualities of public law and most of them showing clear signs of a life of their own, inherent and not derived from the concession of the State.

The State may recognise and guarantee (and demand marks for so doing) the life of these societies—the family, the club, the union, the college, the Church; but it no more creates that life than it creates the individual, though it orders his birth to be registered. It is the problem of the future, as Mr. A. L. Smith showed at the close of his lecture on Maitland, to secure from legal theory the adequate

recognition of these facts, and in regard to
religion the problem is raised in an acute
form, and it will be the service of multiplied
sectarianism to a true, that is a realistic
political, philosophy if it forces the recognition of the truth that smaller societies
live by their own life, and exercise real
authority over their members. The struggle
for liberty nowadays is the struggle to
secure that recognition. What I have
tried to indicate is the causes of that
struggle being arduous. The atmosphere
in which law has lived for more than one
millennium (apart from the Teutonic and
feudal influences) has been all in favour of
the doctrine which recognises two and only
two social entities, the individual on the
one hand and the State on the other. In
that atmosphere law not only gets out of
relation to living facts and precipitates
struggles like the *Kultur-kampf* and absur-
dities like those involved in the case of the
Free Church of Scotland, but political
philosophy, which is always largely dependent on law, oscillates between an
unreal individualism and a wildly impossible
socialistic ideal. The facts of life are hostile

P

to both, but injury, both practical and theoretical, is always done by trying to ignore facts, especially facts so tremendous as the complex group-life which is to most of us more than the State. What I have tried to show is that this error is not of modern origin, that it did not come into our world at the Renaissance, though it may have been accentuated then, but that it is part of the *damnosa hereditas* from the Civil Law of the Roman Empire, of which Stubbs once said that, whenever it had been dominant, it destroyed any real idea of civil and religious freedom.[1]

[1] I do not claim to have proved the view here set forth; still less to have set out the whole evidence. I am not certain of any hard and fast categories in the topic. But I would ask the student to study the ecclesiastico-political controversies throughout their course, from the *Libelli de Lite* down to the modern newspaper and platform speaker, and to ask himself whether the view here put forward does not fit more readily into the words and modes of thought of thinkers on all sides than that which I have combated.

APPENDIX II

THREE CAMBRIDGE HISTORIANS:
CREIGHTON, MAITLAND, AND ACTON

AND SOME OF THEIR SIGNIFICANCE IN REGARD TO THE PROBLEM

IT was the fortune of the writer to be brought into intimate relations with three of the greatest minds which were occupied about historical matters during the nineteenth century. Now that the youngest of them has passed away it may not be uninteresting to my readers if I make some attempt to compare three men, so original and so different, who among them have done so much for the cause of the historical inquiry and the yet more valuable habit of historical thinking in this country. No attempt will be made to appraise their whole work, for it would be quite beyond the power of the writer and indeed an impertinence. Probably, indeed, the time has not yet come when such appraisement can be made. Maitland's theories, in particular, are many of them hypothetical, and time can only show whether his conjectures will be generally accepted by scholars; although, of course, a great mass of his work has now become a part of our common heritage. But while the personal memory of these great men is still fresh, it may be possible to gather together certain characteristic details which will serve to set them in stronger relief, and to exhibit their relations to one another, and also certain ways in which all three have influenced and will influence in the future the general conception of the Church and its place in society. Perhaps their unity is more apparent in this way than in any other, except that all three were born students, with the enthusiasm of knowledge burning within them. Yet it was not knowledge (even in Maitland's case) entirely apart from life, divorced from all practical affairs. For all three were far more than mere scholars, and at all times were a little irritating to pedants.

At first sight the differences between the

three men are far more striking than their
resemblance. Creighton, incomparably the
greatest man of the three, was a country
clergyman, a don, an ecclesiastic, and,
finally, one of the most successful bishops
of modern times. Maitland, though a
professor, was never in the old sense a
college don, was by profession a barrister,
and in opinions an agnostic with a strongly
anti-clerical bias. Acton was half a German,
a journalist, a courtier, a squire, and, above
all things, a devoted Roman Catholic, with
an intense fear of Ultramontanism. If
Creighton was the greatest man, Maitland
was equally the greatest historian, and
Acton, by general judgment, the most
widely erudite. Again, though all three
were professors at Cambridge, one of them
was trained at Oxford, and preserved all
his life traces of his Oxford manner, although he sent his sons to Cambridge;
Maitland was emphatically Cantabridgian
in sentiment and outlook, and rejoiced to
call himself a disciple of Sidgwick, perhaps
the most characteristically Cambridge mind
of the nineteenth century, if we except his
brother-in-law, Mr. Arthur Balfour; while

Acton's university training took place at
Munich under Döllinger, and developed to
a degree which minimised his influence the
spirit of critical detachment from groups
and parties. Yet all three were alike not
merely in their intellectual ideal, their scorn
of emotion apart from principle, and their
passion for justice, but in their strong
belief in liberty and their perception of the
hollowness of much that goes by the name
nowadays. It is this faith in freedom
which is in different forms the characteristic
of them all, and led to each of them making
contributions towards the solution of one
of the chief problems of our day—the relation between the modern omnicompetent
State and the rights of smaller societies to
exist and to govern themselves within it.
All three, though two of them without
particularly desiring it, have helped, and
will help still more in the future, towards
a true conception of the place of our
Church in regard to Christendom at large,
and also in relation to modern democracy.
In each case this result was assisted by the
special study of the scholar, and each case
affords, therefore, evidence of the value for

practical action, of speculations and research, apparently most remote and even antiquarian.

I.—MANDELL CREIGHTON

Let us take them in order of their going, and try to estimate their special distinctions as teachers and thinkers. Of the many-sided activity of Mandell Creighton it would obviously be impossible to speak within the limits of a short article. Nor is it necessary. For his whole personality is revealed to us not only in his books, but in those incomparable letters which Mrs. Creighton has published in what is one of the half-dozen best biographies in the language. But one or two points may be noted about his teaching. As a lecturer, and still more as private tutor, the main cachet of Creighton's teaching was the constant stimulus he gave to thought and activity. What struck us most was the wide range of his interests, his sense of the absolute importance of knowledge, and, as I once heard him say, " the appalling levity " with which the members of the so-called educated classes deliver opinions on every conceivable topic. It would be truer to say that he tried to make men discipline themselves than that he endeavoured himself to discipline them. Alike in religion, politics, learning, he always respected and believed in the individual. His great object, indeed, was to make the individual believe in himself; not, of course, in the sense of being arrogant or self-conscious. No one could be severer to anything of that sort. But he tried to make his pupils see that there were tasks worthy of their attempting; that they ought not to be afraid of them, and that they must be makers of their own lives. One of the first lessons we learnt from him was the absurdity of worshipping "the idols of the market-place" and the iniquity of satisfying ourselves with plausible hypocrisies and conventional fallacies. No one exposed more unsparingly the superficial sentimentality which often mistakes itself for culture. In the strict sense Creighton was not a great preacher; yet many an undergraduate has learnt through him to see that culture means something different from the catchword of a literary and artistic coterie, that intellectual riches need as much work to win as material, and that, as he said once in a sermon, "a certain self-consciousness that serves for culture" is not the sufficient ideal of a University life.

Of the three men, Creighton was undoubtedly the greatest teacher of youth, and did much to save from being mere dilettanti the interested "literary" youths who abound at the Universities. The fact is, that intellectual sloppiness is a far greater danger than mere athleticism, of the evils of which one hears so much.

After all, athletics in themselves are good, and even those who are exclusively devoted to them are often thereby saved from worse things. But mere playing with intellectual interests, which is the bane of the clever undergraduate, is almost unmitigated evil, and yet it seems an evil far less realised by those who ought to stop it. This, probably, was at the bottom of the method of lecturing, which was a little disjointed, but eminently suggestive. He did not, like Acton and Maitland, deliver, as professor, lectures which were finished compositions and could be published as they stood. Rather, his lectures were interesting monologues, in which new ideas and fresh books were constantly being brought to the mind.

It was by his interest in ideas and extraordinary fertility of mind that he surpassed the other two men. There was no topic to which he did not give a new aspect, no subject into which he did not seem to see deeper than anyone else, no material which he did not illuminate, even though he might have no new fact to tell.

The amazing value of the last volume of his great work on the Papacy has never been adequately recognised. Among the myriad books which deal with the Lutheran outburst, we doubt if there is one which at all approaches Creighton's in the way it envisages the movement. For it exhibits Luther neither as a hero nor a scoundrel, not even as a great religious genius, but as a problem worrying himself and worrying statesmen, but for them, of course, only one of the many sources of perplexity inherent in *la haute politique.* That is the real distinction of the book—that it brings us back into the world of diplomacy and ecclesiastical manœuvring, in which Luther was simply one more of the many nuisances of the working politician's life. Even when they relate the other events in detail, most historians seem unable to prevent the Reformation movement looming as large in their views as it does in the light of its world-historical importance. The difference is in tone rather than in statement, but it is very real, and no one else reproduces the atmosphere of European intrigue and Papal statesmanship with the reality and ease of Creighton. In a way which is almost unique he helps us to re-think the thoughts of the Papal Court or the Imperial chancellors.

From the point of view of this paper, however, it is another point on which I want to insist—Creighton's conception of the Church of England. His most profound research lay in a period scarcely known to Englishmen, yet worthier of study than many of the more picturesque epochs of Church history—the period of the Conciliar movement—roughly speaking, 1378–1450. The interest of this period does not lie in the practical success of the movement, which was little or none, but in the ideas which animated it. Broadly speaking, it may be said that those ideas, and those ideas alone, form the *raison d'être* of the Church of England, as against Ultramontanism on the one hand and individualistic Protestant sectarianism on the other. The claim of Rome that we are but a sect among many other sects would be justified if the Conciliar movement was based on a fundamental falsehood. Roughly speaking, the ideals of Gerson and his congeners were those of a reformed Episcopal communion, with nationalism recognised in the Church as a real thing, with a constitution limiting the dangers of centralised bureaucracy (the real evil of Rome far more than mere monarchical government)—in a word, with federalism in the Church preserving the unity of the whole while securing the independence of the parts. The failure of that scheme is one of the most tragic facts in the history of the world, and was as direct a cause of the Reformation as the despotism of Louis XIV was the real origin of the great Revolution. Now, Creighton's task in later years was to apply this truth to modern problems. There arose in the Church a party small, for the most part unlearned, but intensely enthusiastic, whose ideals were purely those of Latin Christianity, and whose conception of the Church was in the last resort ultramontane.

Creighton saw earlier than most people that the real question at issue was not whether the Church of England had done this or that in the past, not even whether it had the right to do this and that, but whether there was a Church of England at all.

The theory of what is called by some Catholicism (by which is meant that the Church is outwardly a unitary and omni-competent State) ends, if it be pushed to its logical extreme, in the tyranny of the central power, and the complete absorption of all smaller units—its logical issue is the ultra-montane theory of Episcopal jurisdiction, which it makes merely and solely a delega-tion of the Papacy, and it is not really necessary for this theory that the govern-ment should be monarchical; a democratic despotism would be just as bad. The real point is whether National Churches have any real existence. Are they as much the expression of God's will as individual persons? Have they a distinct and peculiar mission to perform, not apart from but in unison with the general body? Creighton strongly maintained that they had inherent rights, powers, and life of their own; and equally strongly maintained that the Church of England in laying down its rules was guided by " an appeal to sound learning." Now, this was eminently the cachet of the Conciliar movement, which represented the culminating point of University influence in the Middle Ages. It can, I think, scarcely be denied that Creighton's advocacy of the rights of nationalism within the Church, and his equally strong repudiation of mere individualism, were, if not a result of his historical investigations, at any rate enormously increased in depth and weight of advocacy by his very peculiar knowledge of that half-forgotten movement.

Here, however, as elsewhere, his respect for liberty preserved him from mistakes. Convinced of the truth of his main principles, imbued as he was perhaps more strongly than any thinker since Hooker with the genius of the Church of England, despising the frivolity and ignorance with

which the Latinisation of the Church was
being pushed forward, and deeply opposed
to the legalist conception of religion in
general, and to "canonist" Christianity in
particular, Creighton's strong hand alone
prevented an outburst of the persecuting
spirit which would have entirely defeated
its own object, and would have left the
Church shorn of some of its best elements.
He felt that the same arguments which
justified religious liberty, in spite of all the
dangers of competing creeds and the emer-
gence of every form of unbelief into articu-
late prominence, would also justify the
attempt to leave dangerous tendencies to
work themselves out rather than by re-
pression to leave the evil smouldering.
Episcopal authority stood very high to his
mind, but he was not prepared to support it
by coercion, if men (committing as he deemed
a sin) refused to bow to that authority.
His cachet as a teacher, as a historian, and as
a bishop, was just this—that no one ever had
a stronger sense of the value of organised
government and the need of authority alike
in Church and State, combined with a
respect for individuality and a belief in

freedom which were of the essence of the man. This, more than anything else, made him a representative of the English Church at its best, and that is the English character at its best. And all this while he preserved a faculty for detailed thought and criticism which made ignorant persons complain that he was flippant and censorious. It was merely "the Englishman's privilege of grumbling" as exercised by a very highly trained intellect in an intelligent and ever alert observer. For while Creighton saw and lamented the defects of his countrymen, as when he said that "Englishmen above all men refuse to think things out," and that "most Englishmen have no mind at all, but only hereditary obstinacy," he owed his powers to his universal sympathy with them, and to being himself emphatically an Englishman, not, like Matthew Arnold, a mere "kid-gloved Jeremiah."

II.—FREDERICK WILLIAM MAITLAND

A very different man from Creighton was Maitland, except in his many-sided activity. For he was no mere recluse interested in nothing but the dry bones of legal history, but one of the foremost men in academic life. For some years he sat on the Council of the Senate—and Maitland was not a man who could be a member of any body without influencing it. With Downing he had no connection until the days of his professoriate, but he took a keen interest in the concerns of the college, even down to the fortunes of its boat. At home, as no one except Stubbs and, perhaps, Mr. Round have ever been, in the " diplomatic " and other records of early English life, he was an admirer of Ibsen, of Meredith, of Anatole France, and an admirable after-dinner speaker. As an historian he was eminently a " path-finder," and has probably done more to revolutionise our ideas of English origins than any one, except Stubbs and, possibly, Liebermann. His interests were precisely opposite to those of Creighton. To the latter the personal side of history strongly appealed, and while there is no trace in either writer of any striving after what is picturesque and dramatic, it is evident that the analysis of character takes a foremost place in the

Q

method of Creighton, while it is the development of institutions that normally interests Maitland. The latter cares for the structure of civilised life, its juridical skeleton and economic basis; the former for the men who work upon the structure, for the manipulators of institutions, for the diplomatist and the statesman. Not that Maitland is ever dry, or that Creighton is always vivid. Both are alike in this, that they enlarged the horizons of all cultivated Englishmen. Creighton's interest was primarily European, and even Italian; his book, incidentally, is a better history of the Renaissance than the pretentious volubility of Symonds. It is the theatre of European statecraft at the period of transition from the dream of mediæval unity to the reality of modern nationalism that Creighton loved to gaze upon, and so to raise his readers above the narrow and insular view of history which is characteristic of so many Englishmen.

Maitland had a similar feeling, in spite of the fact that his work lay almost exclusively in the origins of English legal and constitutional life. I heard him criticise a scheme

for historical teaching on the ground that it
was "far too English." He desired that
youths should be trained to see history
from a standpoint not of their own nation,
which is comparatively easy to attain, but
of the best science of Germany, and perhaps even more of France. For although
Maitland's studies were emphatically directed
to find by "slow degrees the thoughts of
our forefathers," "to think once more their
common thoughts about common things,"
he knew very well that this would not be
achieved without an endeavour to correlate
the development of this country to that of
others in Western Europe, insisting not
only on the differences, which are superficial, but on the resemblances, which, at
least up to the fourteenth century, are
essential and profound. Creighton and
Maitland and Acton were in fact at work
on one problem—the development of the
modern Western mind and its relation to
the sources from which it had proceeded.
Only Creighton envisaged the problem
from the standpoint of the statesman-
ecclesiastic, Maitland from that of a trained
lawyer, and Acton from that of a political

and ethical philosopher. All were alike in that their method was eminently that of historically-minded thinkers; but they differed in standpoint, in opinion, and to some extent in the material each made his own. Maitland—to return to him—more than anyone else is responsible for the annihilation of what may be called the lawyer's view of history, which dates everything from the thirteenth century, and regards the reign of Henry II as equally with that of Henry I in legal twilight. Even before Maitland it had dawned upon a few legal minds that there were great men before Stephen Langton, and that a theory of English land-law and the courts which went little further back than Edward I was not likely to be adequate (except, of course, for the practice of the courts). Just as it needed Freeman, with all his faults, to induce the ordinary historical reader to believe that anything really happened before 1066, so it needed Maitland, with all his genius, to break down the even more intolerable tyranny of insular jurists, and to limit the empire of Coke. There are few passages more illuminating, not only for the English student, but for all those interested in the growth of mediæval institutions on the ruins of the Roman Empire, than the few introductory pages on the nature of feudalism in the *History of English Law* (vol. i. pp. 66–73). The writer, who heard this, or most of it, delivered as a lecture in that small room at Downing on a dark autumn afternoon to a yet smaller audience, is not likely to forget the impression then made.

This brings me to one point about Maitland which might be otherwise neglected— his characteristics as a lecturer. If the main impression given by Creighton was that of intellectual versatility and alertness, of the duty of thinking things out, the main impression of Maitland was that of the paramount importance of what he was talking about. His style was and is like that of no one else, compact of extraordinary Biblical and other archaisms, intensely individual, vivid and striking, packed with allusions, sparkling with humour, and suggesting even more than it stated—the very opposite of the matter-of-fact, unadorned narrative of Creighton as an historian. It was a style like the portrait of Monna Lisa, which all the thoughts and experiences of the world seemed to have moulded, and it had, whether delivered or written, an extraordinary quality, almost unique among historians—that of reproducing the atmosphere of the time he was discussing. It was not descriptive or picturesque in the ordinary sense. There was neither the hardness nor the brilliancy, still less the partisanship, of Macaulay in Maitland's mind. But just as he left his hearers under the impression that there was only one thing worth living for—the study of twelfth-century law—as he discoursed in his vibrating and nervous tones (for he was nervous to the last), so his writing serves to bring before us the mental atmosphere of the men he talks of with a reality quite unlike that of the narrative historian and quite different from the memoir-writer. Perhaps it was best expressed once in the phrase of Mr. Andrew Lang, that he turned flashes of electric light on his subject.

Maitland, in fact, is to the ordinary historian what Mr. Sargent is to the ordinary portrait painter. The genius for life is perhaps the best name for the characteristic

which makes them both so different from
other men, which marks their quality and
limits as well as expands their powers.
Stubbs is a great historian, but he tells us
of a dog that remains dead; Froude is a
great dramatist, but he delights us with
the tragedy of personality. Macaulay paints
pictures. Maitland shows us life, and not
the lives of statesmen merely, but of human
beings. Other men know and we learn
from them. Maitland saw, and we learn
more from him; only what he sees is not
the dress, the buildings, and the accessories
of life, but the inner world of thought
and feeling, "the common thoughts of our
fathers about common things." This is
what I mean by likening him to Sargent,
from whose pictures the genius of the
fevered world he portrays will look out
for ever, for a new Maitland to interpret
in an age yet to come.

Although Maitland was, as no one is
ignorant, not merely a non-Christian, but
an anti-clerical, yet few men have done
more to elucidate Church history. If we
cannot say of him as Newman said of
Gibbon, that he is our greatest ecclesias-

tical historian, it remains that on many important matters, such as the aims of Henry II in regard to criminous clerks, and the nature of English ecclesiastical jurisprudence in the Middle Ages, he has done more than anyone else to clear men's thoughts. Few now are likely to repeat the assertion, dear to the Tractarianism of an obsolete type, that the English Church only accepted the canonical system " by courtesy," and exercised powers not claimed in France or Aragon. Nor must the intellectual ancestry of Maitland be forgotten. A brief glance at his grandfather's writings—*The Dark Ages*, for instance— will show the intelligent observer the true source of much of his manner, and even a little of his method. For S. R. Maitland had a gift of historical imagination which, even by the side of his grandson's genius, is by no means to be despised, and ought never to be ignored in an estimate of the man. Maitland's main contribution to the Church was, however, in this writer's opinion, not in any of his special studies, but is to be found in the Preface of Gierke, which he prefixed to his translation. That

book, the *Deutsche Genossenschaftsrecht*,
he once declared to me to be the greatest
book he had ever read ; and it is possibly
through Gierke's influence more than any
other, that Maitland came to demolish—no
weaker term can be used—the old conception of the position of corporate bodies
in the State. That conception makes all
clubs, associations, communities, religious,
political, or economic, the mere creatures
of the omnicompetent modern State
(which inherits its claims from Imperial
Rome), with no right to exist, except on
concession, express or implied, and no
powers of action beyond what the State
(in theory) delegates to them. This theory
(which if it does not depend on, at least
is connected with the canonist doctrine of
Innocent IV, that the corporation is a
persona ficta) it has been the work of the
German school of " realists " to overthrow.
Gierke, and men like him, looking back
from Roman to Teutonic origins, and
looking out into the facts of the world
to-day, have seen the absurd chaos into
which this theory would land us, and its
utter falsity to life as actually lived, for

it makes the world consist of a mass of self-existing individuals on the one hand and an absolute State on the other; whereas it is perfectly plain to anybody who truly sees the world that the real world is composed of several communities, large and small, and that a community is something more than the sum of the persons composing it—in other words, it has a real personality, not a fictitious one. This is the essence of what is true in modern nationalism, and in the claims for the rights of churches and of trade unions. It was the ground (probably unconscious) of the decision in the Taff Vale case, and also of the law which (practically) reversed the decision and reverted to the mediæval notion of immunities for corporate bodies. The failure to recognise the truth of the personality of communities other than the State was partly at the bottom of the House of Lords' decision in the great case of the Free Church of Scotland, as anyone can see who reads Mr. Haldane's ingenious but unsuccessful effort to induce the Court to apply to the United Free Church the ordinary canons of personal identity. In-

stead of this they said they were considering the body merely as a "trust," thinking
by that to escape all theological discussion,
and being, in consequence, dragged further
and further in the quagmire.

The mention of this latter case illustrates
the point I wish to make—namely, the
importance of this view of the nature of
a community for the claims of the Church.
It is useless for a modern Church to assert
claims merely by Divine right against the
State; it is impossible for it to claim
absolute liberty to do exactly what it likes ;
for the State exists not indeed to found, as
in the old theory, but to control and limit
within the bounds of justice, the activities
of all minor associations whatsoever. The
point of issue is not whether Churches can
do anything they choose, but whether
human law is to regard them as having
inherent powers, rights, and wills of their
own—in a word, a personality. If they
have, their activity might be restrained in
so far as it interferes with others—thus,
they would not be allowed to persecute,
and ought not to be allowed. But they
will have certain rights, such as those of

meeting, excommunication, development of doctrine, and others, which are inherent and not concessionary. I believe that even the education struggle is at bottom a struggle between those who recognise this right and those who do not. And because I believe it to be true about man in society, quite apart from religious interests, I think it certain that in the long run we shall win in this struggle. If we do we shall owe more than many people like to acknowledge to the men who, guided by the pure spirit of disinterested inquiry, and driven by the intellectual passion for truth, inspired not merely the historical but the legal minds of the day with the true, opposed to the false, theory of the place which societies formed for special ends must occupy in the great all-embracing State. The truth is that both the State and the individual as commonly envisaged are not facts but fictions. There is no more dangerous superstition than that political atomism which denies all power to societies as such, but ascribes absolutely unlimited competence over body, soul, and spirit to the imposing unity of the State. It is indeed " the great leviathan " made up of little men, as in Hobbes's title-page, but we can see no reason to worship the golden image which Machiavelli has set up. That worship ends in the Church with Ultramontanism, in the State with Absolutism. We have seen how Creighton's theory of nationalism introduces the true federal element into the notion of the Church. We now see how Maitland's "realism," his doctrine of the inherent powers of corporations, limits the equally dangerous activity of the State. The one work complements the other. One is the justification of Anglicanism in ecclesiastical theory, the other will form the true defence of religious bodies against governmental interference.

III.—LORD ACTON

The third of the three Cambridge professors we are delineating was not the greatest, but he was the most mysterious, and his life the most pathetic of the three. Despite all attempts to explain his career, it remains to most people shrouded in enigma. And despite his academic honours, his European fame, and his peerage, his

life was, on the whole, a failure. While
Creighton's was a success from every point
of view, without his ever being vulgarised
or hardened by success, while Maitland
achieved all that he might reasonably have
expected, and was honoured and loved in
his lifetime in a way more usual to the
charlatan than to the true genius, Acton
was eminently " an inheritor of unfulfilled
renown," never producing any one work
to which his admirers could point, and
failing in the grand practical scheme of his
life—the introduction of true Liberalism
to the Roman Church, and the elimination
(or at least the setting back) of the forces,
always so strong in any religion, that made
for tyranny. None of these three lived to
be an old man, though Acton was the
oldest by ten years. But while the others
did more than most men do in double the
time, and, whether in literature or in life,
could point to a splendid row of achieve-
ments, Acton could show little beyond a few
journalistic enterprises, always ending in
failure owing to the hostility of the Roman
hierarchy; political enthusiasm (the belief
in Irish or Boer nationality) that in their last

and highest expression were destined to defeat; and a religious and moral activity which beat itself in vain against the inexhaustible resources of ultramontane disingenuity and the granite walls of Jesuit intolerance. Such, as it appears to the outside world, are the facts. And even those who cherish most his memory must sorrowfully concede to his numerous detractors that Acton produced no single work that can be called epoch-marking, that he did not succeed in politics, had no aptitude for the compromise which is the essence of our public life, and never for one moment "held the stage." It is not insignificant for English habits that the only place in the Government for a man deep in the counsels of the chief of the party, and knowing more than nearly all the Cabinet put together, should have been that of a Lord-in-Waiting.

Yet, as will be seen when more of his remains are given to the world, his literary output was far larger than people are commonly aware of; while it is possible that when the history of the strange century through which we have just passed is really understood—perhaps it never will be—

Acton's name may stand higher as that of one who really prepared for the future than that of many an empire-builder like Cecil Rhodes, or many an ecclesiastic of the machine like Manning. Manning, be it remembered, was essentially a Boss Croker, and has no other claim to the intellectual remembrance of his country than belongs to the skilled manipulator of other men's abilities, the organiser of victory for a party cause. As the expression of this type at its highest Manning will always be worthy of remembrance, but that jealousy of Newman, which was the main motive of his treatment of the great Cardinal, was only indefensible because it was so superfluous. In the days to come people will not compare the two men to Manning's disadvantage. But they will talk and write of Newman, and think as much of Manning (and as little) as of the Jay Goulds or Schnadhorsts of life, to whose class he essentially belongs. Some will put him higher, some lower, in that class. For some he will merely be a name, like Cardinal Ricci, a name in a biographical dictionary. But he will never in the future be compared with Newman, because you can only compare things that are of the same kind—you cannot compare a rainbow with a popgun. The same is the case with Acton. Manning despised him as the successful trust magnate despises an artist content with a small income, or a rival who allows himself to be thwarted through some scruple about honesty. Yet it is possible that in the days to come it may be found that in the true meaning of the word success—influence on human life towards the noblest—Acton was as much superior to Manning as an honest labourer is to a card-sharper. Nobody knew better than Acton that he had not made all the use men expected of his knowledge. What was it that paralysed his activity? People often say that it was the mere weight of the burden of his knowledge, or the love of accumulation which grew on him, as the handling of gold does upon a miser. I suspect that the cause lay deeper. When he said after the days of the Vatican Council were over that "the present generation are hopeless, he must work for the future," he expressed at once his ground of (comparative) inactivity and the source of his enduring fame. That fame will, I am convinced, rest on two grounds besides the enormous depth and range of his knowledge —first, his absolute insistence on the paramountcy of the moral law in politics, and secondly, his perception of the true theory of liberty as opposed to the pretentious blare of modern Continental Liberalism and the yet more pretentious fallacies of despotism masquerading as democracy.

To compare him for a moment as a lecturer with the two men we have been discussing, Acton's distinction lay in this moral passion. His lectures had not the abundant fertility of suggestion which characterised Creighton, nor had his conversation; he did not, perhaps, so constantly drive one to cross-examine one's ideas. He had not Maitland's gift of historic imagination, and presented the results of study, the fruit of reflection, and not the breathing movement of the times he discussed. He did not make us dig into ourselves like Creighton, nor did he take us out of ourselves like Maitland. Yet in one respect his lectures were more impressive than those of either. Less suggestive than Creighton, less enthralling than Maitland, less humorous and unexpected than either, he excelled them in moral passion and dignity and weight of eloquence. No one could listen to him without being convinced of the tremendous issues which lie in political choice, or of the absolute difference between right and wrong doing. It was this burning conviction of the eternal distinction between good and bad, and the immeasurable gulf that divides expediency from justice, that gave to his lectures, his writings, and his life their peculiar significance. His whole life was, in fact, a protest against the principles of Machiavelli—that is, of purely utilitarian morals, whether in Church or State. He did not deny that public might be different from private morality. What he did deny was that there was no such thing as public morality at all. In the long run either ethical Individualism or Socialism is equally destructive of morals. Individualism *in extremis* is pure anarchy. Socialism— the absolute absorption of individuals by the community—destroys conscience (I am speaking of pure and ethical socialism, not of this or that economic arrangement). Acton, like Creighton, held firmly to the truth on both sides, though the circumstances of his struggle within the Roman Church caused him to lay stress rather on the claims of the individual.

But whoever studies carefully Acton's writings will find that he discerned no less clearly than Creighton or Maitland the nature of the struggle before us, and laid down principles which, in the present writer's judgment, are of paramount—indeed, of indispensable—value in the days that are beginning. His theory of the nature of liberty, that there must be room not only for individual rights but for the rights of self-existing communities within the State, his hatred of the worship of the "mortal god" and the prostration of the soul before the idols of democracy or despotism, can easily be gathered from his papers on *Nationality* and *Political Thoughts on the Church*, in addition to the better-known lectures on the *History of Freedom*. The decisive phrase in his statement that while the modern State allows individuals to

choose their own Church, it will not allow
the Church to rule itself and have its own
laws, is being proved now by events in
France, as it was effectively demonstrated
by Bismarck's attitude in the *Kultur-kampf*,
and can be found illustrated in the utterances of many English politicians at the
present moment. His theory of liberty
was at bottom the same as that of Creighton, and was based politically upon Burke
and the great theorists of Whiggism. As
he was careful to point out, it was by no
means identical with, indeed was strongly
opposed to, modern " Liberalism." Despite
the supposed unorthodoxy of his position
as a Roman Catholic, no one else has condemned Cavour and the policy of the Italian
Government in such severe terms—the more
unsparing in that they are based upon a
reasoned principle of political philosophy,
and not upon prejudice or passion.

The other element in Acton that is of
importance, namely his perception that the
true notion of liberty is essentially Christian,
was the possession of the Catholic Church in
its earlier phases, was obscured by Papalism

and denied by Luther, and would come by
its own again when the mists of the past
thousand years had rolled away.   Like Dr.
Inge, he felt that Christianity was still "a
very young religion," that there was no
more need to despair because it had lost
for a few hundred years the true principles
of politics, than because for a moment " the
world had found itself Arian."   To us, of
course, this position is the strongest possible justification of Anglicanism, and recent
events are forcing Churchmen of different
schools to see this.   Like many other
Churches, our Church has made in the
past the mistake of asking for worldly
power instead of religious freedom, and
she is now reaping the fruit of that error.
But first the education question, then probably the marriage problem, and, it may
be later, doctrinal and other matters will
drive Churchmen to claim, not the support
of the State against other creeds, as in old
days of uniformity, not even social prestige
as against dissent, as is sometimes the case
to-day, but the right to " live and let live,"
confident that in the long run liberty can

never injure the cause of truth, and that
a Church which dispenses with every form
of appeal to lower motives will make up
by intensity of enthusiasm in its members
for any diminution of strength in their
numbers. The theory of liberty is always
concerned at bottom with human character,
and is based upon the belief that it is more
important that men should do right from
proper motives than that their external
actions should be correct. Acton's position
as a member of a body but recently persecuted in his native land, and as a protagonist of a cause oppressed within his own
Church, enabled him to see the truth more
clearly than most men. His knowledge of
the past helped him to correlate it with the
conflicts of the Church against a Pagan or
non-Christian State in earlier ages. His belief
in the future led him to hope that not indeed
till after many struggles and difficulties,
but, none the less, decisively, at last the
true principles of liberty would be realised
in a State controlling but not oppressing
Churches, nations, sects, communities within
it, preventing mutual injustice, while recog-

nising their inherent life, and by a Church once more awakened to the true claims of justice, in which neither should the individual be oppressed by a centralised bureaucracy, nor should mere personal caprice usurp the functions of order and authority. This ideal we of the English Church may well feel is more likely to be realised through our peculiar heritage of English liberty and universal order than in any other way. Indeed, it is the conviction of some of us that one of the main tasks before our Church is to realise this herself, and to cause its recognition at once by the State and by other nations. That Acton did not see it is no more wonderful than that Maitland distrusted all religious organisations (for all have given ground for the mistrust of scientific men), just as the reliance on " the Establishment " and its attendant snobbery would naturally arouse contempt in a man brought up as was Acton. But the fact remains that Acton and Maitland, who did not, no less that Creighton, who did, discern the logical result and visible embodiment of their conceptions, will all alike have contributed towards the recognition of truth in regard to societies within the nation, and all alike have done something to make more secure, because better understood and self-realised, the claims and nature " of this Church and realm."

INDEX

ABSOLUTISM, development of, in sixteenth and seventeenth centuries, 147-9

Acton, Lord, 56, 229-230, 253-265

Quoted on Ultramontanes of early nineteenth century, 110-12

American Revolution caused by claim to Parliamentary omnipotence, 82

Arcana imperii, 79

Arrangements within societies not legally enforceable, 105

Associations Cultuelles rejected by the Pope, 26

Austin and his doctrine of the State, x, 13 ff., 79, 83, 195

Authority:

Nature of, in a society, 158 ff.

of creeds, 163-4

Two dangerous theories of, in English Church, 168

Ultramontane view of, 165

BALDUS, 195

Balfour, Mr. A. J., quoted, 160

Bartolus, viii, 137, 208-9

Bellarmine, 138

Beseler, George, 77 *n.*

Bismarck, Prince, and *Kultur-kampf*, 29-31

Boniface VIII, 80, 106-7, 143, 209

Bossuet, *Defensio Cleri Gallicani*, 157

CALVIN'S *Institutes*, 141

Canon Law—relation to Civil Law, 207

Carlyle, history of Political Theory, 223

Catholicity, nature of, 165-6

Church:

and State, origin and growth of, distinction as to societies, 215-18

Claims to liberty misunderstood, 105-6

Her claims, 4, 37-8

Thought dangerous, 91

Printed by BALLANTYNE, HANSON & Co.
at Paul's Work, Edinburgh